The Path to Holiness

Becoming a Living Sacrifice of Love

The Path to Holiness

Becoming a Living Sacrifice of Love

By

John Paul Thomas

My Catholic Life! Inc.

www.mycatholic.life

ISBN-13: 978-1541004184

ISBN-10:1541004183

INTRODUCTION

What is the most glorious act you could accomplish in life? This question may be answered in many and varied ways, but there is only one good answer. Ultimately, living a life fully immersed in the sacrificial love of Christ is the answer. We are called to become a "Living Sacrifice of Love." The path to that goal centers on the virtues of humility, trust and mercy.

Living a life of ongoing sacrificial love requires you to become a beacon of mercy in this world. Unfortunately, we live in a world that is in many ways void of mercy. It is a world in which harshness and judgment are the norm. However, one of the primary reasons so many people lack mercy in our day and age is because they lack humility and trust.

We also live in a world filled with suffering. But sadly, suffering is rarely understood as an opportunity to achieve the highest level of holiness. Suffering is rarely transformed into sacrificial living. Instead, it is often experienced only as a burden to be avoided.

The goal of this book is to offer you an invitation to look more deeply at the path to holiness and to discover the way in which you can travel it in your own life. This invitation is not simply given to help you grasp the theology of holiness; rather, it is an invitation to live it.

Holiness requires a very radical choice. You cannot become holy by being mediocre in your faith. It is not possible to be humble, trusting and merciful unless you are willing to change your life completely. That may seem frightening at first. Nevertheless, making the "frightening" choice to embark on the path to radical holiness is not only for the great saints, it is a choice that the sinner must also make.

The path to holiness begins by embracing and living the virtues of humility, trust and mercy. From there, the humble, trusting and merciful soul is capable of living sacrificially in that it is capable of uniting all suffering to the Cross of Christ to share in the good fruits of that sacrifice. This book will begin by exploring these following three virtues as the solid foundation for holy and sacrificial living:

1) **Humility:** the virtue opposite to pride that enables you to turn your eyes from yourself to the Lord and upon others. It enables you to become detached from selfish *ambition* and attached to <u>selfless</u> *giving*. Humility opens the door to trust in your life because it enables you to turn to the source of all mercy with abandon and confidence.

2) **Trust:** the virtue that is greatly helped by a humble heart, in that the humble heart does not presume to rely upon itself for strength and mercy. God is the source of everything that is good in life. Therefore, turning to Him with total abandon is the only way to obtain mercy. Simply put, "trust" means one relies upon God for all things rather than oneself.

3) **Mercy:** the result of humbly putting all one's trust in God. Mercy first includes its *reception* from the Heart of Christ and then its *distribution* to others. What a grace this is!

It is much easier to understand the beauty of humility and trust than it is to actually humble yourself and put your complete trust in God. It is much easier to speak about mercy than it is to embrace and live it. In fact, entering into these glorious virtues will be quite painful as the Lord strips away pride, selfishness, fear, doubt and many other vices.

Once you are on the path to holiness and are seeking to live the virtues of humility, trust and mercy, do not be surprised if you are also invited to embrace a life of great suffering in a sacrificial way. Think of Jesus. He was perfect, yet the culmination of His ministry was death on a cross. We are called to this same embrace of the Cross of Christ.

We ultimately become a "Living Sacrifice of Love" when every experience we encounter in life, be they joys or sorrows, are encountered with unwavering virtue as we live fully united to the Cross of Christ. Obtaining this high ideal requires a wholehearted commitment to become more fully transformed into the persons God wants us to be.

Read this book slowly and take it one step at a time. Stay with it, pondering the messages that are shared, looking into your own heart with honesty, and striving to change as you do so. Take small steps and you will find yourself on the path to holiness and a life of radical transformation in Christ.

The abundant mercy of God awaits you! Receiving His mercy and becoming an instrument of mercy for others is the most glorious and satisfying experience you can have in life. Commit yourself to the demanding path of holiness and you will be grateful you did for all eternity.

1

Making the Case for Holiness

Why would you want to seek holiness? Moreover, what exactly does that mean? On a theoretical level, becoming holy sounds intriguing, inviting, mysterious and admirable. However, do YOU want to become holy?

Too often, when faced with that question, the first thing that comes to mind is, "What will I have to give up?" Holiness is often seen in a negative way, meaning those who are holy are often seen as admirable people who have given up most of what is "fun" in life.

When you think of someone who is holy, who comes to mind first? A famous saint? A humble priest? A cloistered nun? A loving aunt or grandma? Whoever comes to mind, they are often seen as good people we admire but have chosen not to imitate. Why is that?

The goal of this first chapter is to make the case that holiness is something that <u>you </u>want to strive to attain. In fact, it is something that you <u>deeply</u> want to achieve, whether you realize it or not. No, achieving a life of holiness is not easy. It's not a life filled with "doing what you want because you want to do it." Goals like that are very superficial and are never fully achievable.

We are all made with an innate desire for happiness. The problem is that most often we become confused as to how we achieve the happiness we desire. Some constantly dream of becoming rich. However, think about it honestly. If you won $100 million dollars, would that make you happy? Perhaps that is hard to answer, because, on the surface, this may be very desirable. Think about all you could do with such riches!

The truth, however, is that all the money in the world will not make you happier. There have even been various in-depth studies that have shown that people who win the lottery actually do not achieve a greater degree of happiness. Sure, lots of money may relieve a certain amount of stress, make life easier in some ways and allow you to do many fun things. However, at the end of the day, neither money, fame, prestige, success nor anything else this world holds in high esteem will make you happier in the truest sense.

Think also of the deception that "fame" will make you happy. For example, if you were a famous actor, a powerful politician or a prominent entrepreneur, would your status equate to instant fulfillment in life? Again, there will always be a certain level of satisfaction that comes with success and fame, but it is not very deep and will leave you wanting only more.

Some years ago there was an interview written in a national paper with a very famous actress from Hollywood. In that interview, the actress shared that she often goes back to her hotel room after large parties and suddenly finds herself feeling very lonely. One would think that if you were a famous actress coming home from one of the best social gatherings in Hollywood you'd be feeling pretty good, not lonely.

However, happiness is not something that the world can give. It never comes with riches, fame or worldly success. It's something much deeper and can be obtained by anyone.

Some years ago, a seminarian from the United States spent the summer in a foreign country learning the language and culture. He spent one week in a very poor country village where many homes had dirt floors. One day, one of the local farmers engaged the seminarian in conversation. The seminarian had spent the week feeling bad about the poverty in which the locals lived, so he wasn't prepared for what the farmer said to him. The farmer looked at him, smiled and said, "You poor Americans! You have so many things and are always so busy with life. Look at me! I have everything I could want. I spend the day with my sheep and in my fields. I have a wonderful family and all that I could want." The seminarian went away from that conversation surprised yet intrigued at how this elderly man pitied him for his material wealth and social status!

What is true happiness? Simply put, happiness is holiness. Holiness is the only way to complete fulfillment in life. Nothing else can come close to satisfying the deep longing you feel in your heart. As Saint Augustine famously said, "Our hearts are restless until they rest in You, oh Lord." Do you find that your heart is restless at times? Do you find that there is something missing in your life? What is it? What can fill that void that you feel?

Defining Holiness

If you can accept the fact that holiness is what makes you happy, the next most important question is this: What does it mean to be holy? Is holiness simply a life of pious devotions, going to church all the time, staying out of trouble, being nice to everyone and being an all-around good person? Maybe it is to a certain extent, but that is a very simplistic definition of holiness, which also fails in its complete accuracy.

True holiness, in its deepest form, requires a profound definition. It means you have humbly surrendered every part of your life to God, have given of yourself freely to others without reserve, have chosen to embrace all suffering in life with love, have chosen to unite it to the Cross of Christ, and have chosen to abandon everything this world offers as good, choosing instead the riches of Heaven. Sound inviting? Perhaps not at first. However, if you understood these defining qualities of holiness, you would desire them with all your soul. But if that definition of holiness is a bit too much at first, don't worry just yet. That very profound definition will be unpacked carefully and thoroughly for the rest of this book.

Furthermore, holiness is found in selfless living. Being selfless is difficult for most people because of our tendency toward selfishness. Think of the two year old child who is asked to share his candy with his brother. A two year old has not yet overcome selfishness and, therefore, will not find much satisfaction in giving his candy away. Sadly, many of us never mature toward selflessness in life, choosing instead to remain spiritual "toddlers."

Recall these words of Jesus, "For whoever wishes to save his life will lose it, but whoever loses his life for my sake will save it" (Luke 9:24). "Losing" our lives means we learn to overcome selfishness and choose, instead, to give ourselves to others without counting the cost. Only when we do this do we *discover* who we are and *become* who we were made to be. In other words, when you actively live in a selfless way, two things happen. First, you "discover" your very self. You discover what it means to be human according to the design of God. God made you to be selfless, and it is only in the act of being selfless that you discover this profound truth of who you are. Second, as you discover who you were made to be, you also become that person. By acting in a selfless way, you become selfless and, thus, you become more fully human in the sense that you become who God made you to be. This process of self-discovery and self-transformation is eye-opening and glorious!

For example, recall the familiar Christmas story of Ebenezer Scrooge. In that story, Ebenezer lived a very self-centered life in which his only concern was for himself and his riches. After his nighttime encounter with the ghosts of Christmas past, present and future, his eyes were opened. He woke up realizing that giving of himself to others and putting the needs of others first was what he was missing in life. As a result, his newly discovered life of charity toward others filled him with the utmost happiness. In that story, Ebenezer discovered who he was made to be and became who he was by his acts of selfless charity. This form of discovery is one that we must all seek to make if we are to discover the purpose of our lives and become holy.

Holiness also means that we allow the hardships of life and all the suffering we endure to become a source of union with God rather than an obstacle in our relationship with Him. This is no easy task! When we suffer we are immediately tempted toward selfishness and tend to look only at the wounds we have received. For example, if someone has a very painful toothache, it may be difficult to think about others in the midst of the pain. But suffering and holiness are not actually opposed to each other. And for that reason, suffering and happiness are not opposed to each other. On the contrary, suffering can actually become a source of the greatest fulfillment in life when it is transformed by grace.

Think about our Lord's life. He lived holiness in human form to its perfection and is, therefore, its perfect model. He was God. He was filled with every virtue and loved all people in an unconditional way. However, He was ultimately hated by many, was persecuted and was murdered. Yet through it all, He accepted every suffering without hesitation, transforming it into an act of sacrificial love.

The insightful question is this: Was Jesus happy in this world? Did the suffering He endured steal away His human fulfillment? These are very important questions to answer. In truth, Jesus took deep delight in being able to give of Himself in a totally selfless way, accepting persecution and death unjustly, transforming it into sacrificial love, and finding great happiness in the process. Though this last statement is packed with deep meaning, we should know that Jesus was perfectly happy in life. In fact, His joy increased as He was invited, by the will of the Father, to sacrifice His life for the salvation of the world. The suffering and persecution He endured did not decrease His happiness. Rather, it had the effect of increasing His happiness on account of the fact that He embraced His suffering in love. When love becomes your response to persecution and other forms of suffering, your soul is transformed and made more fully into the likeness of Christ. It is this transformation that brings about a depth of fulfillment in life that cannot be equaled.

Yes, Jesus was divine. Therefore, it may be hard to believe that you can imitate His example and fully share in His likeness. However, that is exactly what you are called to do in life. You are called to "be perfect" as God Himself is perfect (see Matthew 5:48). If you can believe that Jesus' life is the ideal you are to imitate, then you are ready to start down the path to holiness.

From Your Head to Your Heart

It is much easier to believe what you should do than to do what you believe. Our minds can often grasp the ideal, but our will often struggle in choosing that ideal. However, understanding the two-step process is helpful.

Believing comes first. Your mind must first seek to grasp the ideal you are called to imitate. You must seek to understand the perfection of the life of Christ as your model. You must ponder the will of God and grasp the life of virtue He has chosen for you by the example He set.

However, *knowing* God and His holy will is only the first step. From there, you must let what you have come to know through faith move into your will so that your heart can change. As your convictions of faith move from your head to your will, you are strengthened to choose and live the will of God. It is only when the human will is conformed to the will of God that you begin to become holy. With the transformation of your will, your heart is filled with the presence of God. PRACTICE

IMPLEMENT

By analogy, imagine you want to lose weight. As a result, you spend a few weeks reading up on all of the latest weight loss programs. In that time, you become somewhat of an expert on what works and what doesn't. You study the reviews of many forms of dieting and even buy the right foods and dietary supplements. But learning about weight loss is much different than losing weight. In order for all the information you have studied about the best weight loss programs to bear fruit in your life, you have to start to live those programs.

So it is with holiness. The transition of the will of God from your head to your will is not easy. It requires much virtue and much conversion. It can only be done one step at a time. However, if you choose to embark on that journey, and continue down that road, you will begin to see progress as your life is transformed.

One of the most important ways we begin this journey is through concrete and practical steps. We must examine the mind and will of God in detail. We must then evaluate our own minds in the light of this revelation and we must allow grace to change our thinking, our actions and ultimately our hearts, desires, passion and even feelings.

The Path of No Return

An important initial decision on your part is to make the choice to embark on the "path of no return." Recall Jesus' words, "No one who sets a hand to the plow and looks to what was left behind is fit for the kingdom of God" (Luke 9:62). If you can agree with the basic premise that you were made for holiness and that holiness is the path to human fulfillment and, therefore, the path to happiness, then make the commitment to seek to obtain it. Seek to obtain a life of holiness and use the practical reflections that follow as guideposts on that journey.

this litany, you will be invited to understand this virtue in a very practical way so as to more easily enable you to choose it.

The Litany of Humility

O Jesus! meek and humble of heart, *Hear me.*

From the desire of being esteemed, *Deliver me, Jesus.*

From the desire of being loved, *Deliver me, Jesus.*

From the desire of being extolled, *Deliver me, Jesus.*

From the desire of being honored, *Deliver me, Jesus.*

From the desire of being praised, *Deliver me, Jesus.*

From the desire of being preferred to others, *Deliver me, Jesus.*

From the desire of being consulted, *Deliver me, Jesus.*

From the desire of being approved, *Deliver me, Jesus.*

From the fear of being humiliated, *Deliver me, Jesus.*

From the fear of being despised, *Deliver me, Jesus.*

From the fear of suffering rebukes, *Deliver me, Jesus.*

From the fear of being calumniated, *Deliver me, Jesus.*

From the fear of being forgotten, *Deliver me, Jesus.*

From the fear of being ridiculed, *Deliver me, Jesus.*

From the fear of being wronged, *Deliver me, Jesus.*

From the fear of being suspected, *Deliver me, Jesus.*

That others may be loved more than I, *Jesus, grant me the grace to desire it.*

That others may be esteemed more than I, *Jesus, grant me the grace to desire it.*

That, in the opinion of the world, others may increase and I may decrease, *Jesus, grant me the grace to desire it.*

That others may be chosen and I set aside, *Jesus, grant me the grace to desire it.*

That others may be praised and I unnoticed, *Jesus, grant me the grace to desire it.*

That others may be preferred to me in everything, *Jesus, grant me the grace to desire it.*

That others may become holier than I, provided that I may become as holy as I should, *Jesus, grant me the grace to desire it.*

Anyone who sincerely prays this prayer will be struck by its power and challenged by its content. Humility is no easy task! It is not something you can simply decide to do one day and accomplish the next. True humility requires great surrender and detachment in life. In addition, it requires much grace.

This litany reveals three essential attributes of humility. First, you must be purified of *selfish desires.* Second, you must be purified of *selfish fears.* Third, *selfless desires must increase* in your heart. If you are willing to allow your desires and fears to become transformed by God, you will begin to discover a new freedom from the subtle tendencies of selfishness. The journey may be challenging, but the rewards are glorious.

Purification of Selfish Desires

Do you desire to be esteemed, loved, extolled, honored, praised, preferred to others, consulted and approved? Honestly, unless you are already a saint, then you will most likely discover that these selfish desires are alive in your heart. In fact, most people may respond by saying, "Yes, I desire these 'good' things! Why shouldn't I?" Perhaps you even find yourself surprised that these desires are selfish at all.

The above desires are seen by many as ideals to aim for rather than as sins of pride to be avoided. However, how does God see them? What is the truth about these desires? Let us look at each one of them to paint the picture of humility. If one or more of the sections that follow especially affects you, read it more than once and spend time with it before moving on.

From the desire of being esteemed, deliver me Jesus:

Within the secular world, growing in the esteem of others is often seen as a key to success and advancement in numerous ways. Gaining status and recognition produces prestige and notoriety. It means you have earned people's respect and admiration for what you have done or who you are. So what is wrong with this? The answer is in the <u>desire</u>, not in the fact of being esteemed. In the business world, for example, striving to gain recognition to better market your product or services is quite common and necessary at times. However, there is a difference between working to achieve success within a business (or other daily endeavors) and taking your *personal identity* in that success or failure. Even the most "successful" person must strive for personal humility and the purification of his or her desires. Therefore, to make steps toward humility, the main areas to examine are your <u>personal desires</u> and <u>personal identity</u>.

For example, Saint Mother Teresa was highly esteemed by almost everyone and that esteem opened the door for her to produce an abundance of good fruit through her Christian service. Her heart of radiant love and compassion shone so brightly that she was respected by Christians and non-Christians, by presidents and kings, by the poor and the rich and by saints and sinners. However, Mother Teresa was also exceptionally humble. One key to her humility was that she did not do what she did *so as* to gain the esteem of others. She was not trying to climb the ladder of social notoriety for selfish reasons or so as to *feel* as though she had personal value. Rather, she was exceptionally free from the <u>desire</u> for esteem even though she was, in fact, greatly esteemed by many. So again, humility is found in the purification of the desire, not in the fact of being esteemed.

Think about this carefully. Imagine you did something that thrust you into the public spotlight and led many to hold you in high esteem. Would this satisfy you? Would this make your life better? Would this fulfill you and make you happy on the deepest level? Be careful before you answer those questions. The truth is that even though it may feel good to be admired and respected, those feelings are passing and should not become the foundation of your happiness in life.

Conversely, imagine that you worked very hard at something but your work was perceived by most people as a complete failure. How would that perception affect you? Would the lack of respect and admiration be the cause of your unhappiness and cast you into despair, anger and depression?

Naturally speaking, our fallen human nature tends to care much about what others think of and say about us. However, what should concern us? The humble person cares little about whether another thinks highly of them. But make sure you understand that statement correctly. Sure, it is healthy when someone sees authentic goodness in you, identifies that goodness, and even compliments you because of true virtue. But this recognition ought not to be sought out so as to build up your own self-image. You must never allow yourself to be controlled by the opinions of others, even when they have good opinions of you. Rather, praise from others should be accepted humbly when it is true simply because it is true. Additionally, it is good for the other person to see authentic goodness in you and to rejoice in it. Your primary joy, then, is a result of another person perceiving authentic virtue in your soul and lovingly acknowledging it. However, your worth is not found in the esteem of others or lack thereof. It is found in God and how He sees you.

On the other hand, if someone does not have esteem for you or is highly critical and condemning, humility enables you to listen to what they say and, if there is merit to it, rejoice in the insight given to you by their criticism. If there is no merit to what they say or think, then their criticism must not affect your peace. Criticism will negatively affect you when you struggle with pride and when you have an unhealthy desire for the esteem and praise of others. However, criticism will not affect you when you truly have a humble heart that frees you from the burdensome desires for the praise and esteem of others. Humility is freeing and makes you content only believing the truth of who you are in the mind of God.

From the desire of being loved, deliver me Jesus:

Do you want to be loved? Of course you do! This is a natural desire and is central to your human nature. You were made to give and receive love. So why would you want to be freed from the desire of being loved? The answer requires a very subtle distinction.

Love is not something that you can demand or expect. Love, if it is authentic, must be freely given and freely received. Therefore, it is good to desire authentic love, given freely and in a selfless way. However, the "desire" for this form of love is not a selfish desire. It is <u>not</u> a desire that leads you to say, "I *want* your love because I *need* to be loved by you." Rather, it is a desire that leads you to say, "If you freely choose to offer your love to me...thank you! I am most humbled and grateful." Authentic Christian love cannot be demanded, expected or required of another person. Therefore, when you pray to be delivered from the "desire" of being loved, you are praying to be freed from a desire for selfish love. Interestingly, if you have a selfish desire for the love of another, it can never be fulfilled. Selfishness simply cannot satisfy us. The only authentic way to enjoy the love of another is to first be purified of the desire for that love. Then, and only then, will love be experienced for what it is: a freely given gift for which your only response is gratitude.

In the reception of such a gift, it is normal for a person to allow their *unselfish* desire to receive the love of another. However, they will not depend upon it in a selfish way, demand it, or even expect it. Even among spouses, there must remain a healthy detachment so that the other remains completely free from pressure to offer a true and pure love. Perhaps that is difficult to comprehend, but if you understand that true love must be <u>freely given</u>, then you will better understand that freedom from the *desire for love* actually helps to free others to offer you their love. Only when love is freely offered to you, and not demanded by you, will you be in a position to open your whole being to receive another's gift of love. Love that is freely offered to you by another will even consume and satisfy your healthy and holy desires. However, your desires will not attempt to demand this form of love from another. Instead, your desires will only rejoice in this form of love.

From the desire of being extolled, honored, praised, deliver me Jesus:

Similar to being esteemed are the desires of being extolled, honored and praised. If you have these desires, then you desire more than the esteem of others, you also desire to have that esteem proclaimed in a public way. This reveals an even deeper attachment to the opinions of others.

The person who desires to be extolled, honored and praised struggles with taking their self-worth in the public image that is portrayed about them by others. One danger in this is that if this person is publically criticized, it can become devastating to them. In addition, when they are praised and honored by others in a public way, they feel as though their value has increased. Sadly, by embracing these selfish desires, they become dependent upon the spoken opinions of others. That is a heavy burden to carry for the person because it leads to anxiety, fear, worry, anger and the like.

This selfish desire also leads a person to live on a very superficial level. It produces a disingenuous cover that is easily seen through by others and it often produces a sincere disrespect that others secretly have of them. The praise that they may receive or, at very least, the praise that they seek is nothing more than mere public flattery and lacks a clear depth of truth. Nevertheless, as long as they are flattered, they are "happy" in a superficial way.

The humble person is able to hear and accept the praise of others and rejoice in any truth that is spoken simply because what is spoken is authentic and is an act of love. They rejoice *not* because they are being publically praised; rather, they rejoice because they are being freely loved by another. In this case, their joy is more about the goodness of the other and the love that they share than it is about any compliments they receive.

Take the perfect example of our Blessed Mother. When she visited Elizabeth, Elizabeth cried out "Most blessed are you among women, and blessed is the fruit of your womb" (Luke 1:42). She went on to say, "Blessed are you who believed that what was spoken to you by the Lord would be fulfilled" (Luke 1:45). Elizabeth proclaimed Mother Mary as "blessed" and offered her great praise. Our Blessed Mother, for her part, did not come to Elizabeth seeking this honor or seeking to be extolled by her. However, she did receive this praise since it was true. Humility rejoices in what is true and then responds by offering all praise to God for that truth. Thus, our Blessed Mother's response to the praise of Elizabeth was a song of praise to God: "My soul proclaims the greatness of the Lord; my spirit rejoices in God my Savior. For he has looked upon his handmaid's lowliness; behold, from now on will all ages call me blessed…" (Luke 1:46-48ff).

From the desire of being preferred to others, Jesus deliver me:

A classic example of the desire of being preferred to others is found on the playground at any school. When kids organize a game and they begin to pick sides, almost every child desires that he/she be picked first. The longer one sits waiting to be picked, the more humiliated one feels.

This is quite understandable since children most often have not yet become free from selfishness. In fact, becoming free from selfishness, and in this case the selfish desire of wanting to be preferred to others, is part of the normal process of growing in maturity. Little by little, every child must strive to overcome the struggle of feeling excluded, rejected, less important, and the like. Each must work to rise above these self-image struggles and become free from them. This is part of growing in an authentic and healthy self-image.

So it is with all of us. The humble truth is that it does not matter if others prefer you or not. There is one thing that matters: What does God think of you? This is the only measure that you should use to look at your life.

With that said, it is important to gently confront all selfish tendencies you have. The question to ponder is this: Why would I desire to be preferred to others? The answer is that the person who struggles with this desire has allowed him/herself to take their self-worth <u>in</u> the preference of another. Therefore, they see themselves through the lens of the preference or rejection of another. If they are preferred, then they feel happy and feel as though they have value. If they are not preferred, then they are sad and feel as though they have less value. Again, this is a false measure of one's value and is something each person should humbly seek to avoid.

Hopefully, putting it this way helps you to see the foolishness of such a tendency. Your value is not contingent upon the preference or rejection of another. Sure, it may be personally affirming on a superficial level if someone seeks you out above others. However, if this happens it should not affect your self-image, nor should the opposite experience. Being preferred is fine, but basing your self-worth on it is not.

The humble person, when sought out before others and when preferred to others, will look at this preference as a call to serve and give themselves more fully to those who choose them. They will discover in this act a humble duty to respond to the request of another for the good of the other. It will be seen as a duty of love and service.

From the desire of being consulted, Jesus deliver me:

When another asks for your advice on a difficult topic, this can feel quite affirming. The humble person will encounter such a request as a "holy burden" in the sense that they feel the weight and responsibility to enter into the other person's life or struggle to help them sort things out. This act must be seen as a holy duty and, therefore, a "burden" only insofar as it is a wonderful responsibility and must be embraced with understanding and care. This duty leads you to focus on the person seeking your counsel, not on the self-affirmation you may be tempted to feel by being consulted.

On the other hand, just as in the above-mentioned situation, if a person were to seek out and desire the act of being consulted for a reason such as feeling important, this would be an act of pride. In that case, the consultation becomes more of a selfish act than an act of love and care for the other.

This is important to understand if you want your goal in life to be the authentic and humble care of others. It's good to be consulted if you can sincerely use that opportunity to give your mind, heart, compassion and concern to the other. In this case, you must seek to be an instrument of the truth of God as well as the mercy of God. However, the most important guiding principle is that your actions will be centered on the other, not on yourself. The consultation another seeks from you will result in an act of charity on your part and both will benefit from this act.

From the desire of being approved, Jesus deliver me:

The desire of being approved should already be understood clearly for what it is, based on the above reflections. Again, you must be careful not to take your identity in the approval or disapproval of another person. You must daily seek only the approval of God. Therefore, when you fail, you must rejoice in the discovery of your failure so that this discovery will become a means of change in your life. When you succeed in acting in accord with the will of God, you must rejoice in the discovery of your union with God's will and take satisfaction in this alone.

It is also important to point out the subtle fact that when someone approves of you and your actions, you should not immediately accept what they say or think. This is not intended to sound harsh but, in a sense, it doesn't matter what another thinks of you, or if they approve of you. All that matters is what is true. However, you can find value in the approval or disapproval of others if you are humble. The humble soul will use the convictions of others as a source of its own examination of conscience. Thus, if you are humble and your sin is pointed out to you, you will rejoice in this discovery and strive to change. On the other hand, if you are praised for something that is not of God, you will proceed with caution and not accept that approval into your heart.

In the end, the experience of being approved or not approved must lead you to turn your eyes to the good of the other and to the truth in the mind of God. When you accept the words of another as being true, you must return gratitude to the person as an act of love. When you experience another's words as false, you must see this as an opportunity to help guide the person back to the truth. Thus, the humble soul is always looking out for the good of the other. It is in this act of selflessness that the humble soul discovers who it is in the light of truth.

Purification of Unhealthy Fear

The first part of the "Litany of Humility" focuses on the purification of pride that leads to selfish desires. The second part of the Litany turns to the purification of pride that leads to unhealthy fear. It may not be immediately apparent that fear is the result of certain forms of pride, and it may not be immediately apparent that humility casts out unhealthy fear, but that's exactly what happens. What a wonderful motivation this is to grow in humility—freedom from fear.

Why is humility the remedy for fear? Because fear manifests itself in our lives when we are self-absorbed, tending only to focus in on ourselves. When this happens, we experience certain effects of self-absorption such as becoming disturbed, worried, paranoid, angry, fearful and the like.

Of course there are some forms of healthy fear. For example, if you were to stand on the edge of a cliff and look over, you may be immediately overwhelmed with a form of fear stemming from the natural tendency of self-preservation. In this case, the natural fear that arises within you acts as a safeguard against falling off the cliff. This is a good fear to have.

However, other forms of fear tend to be more selfish and are motivated by a form of pride. Below are some areas of fear that we must seek to eradicate from our lives if we are to grow in humility.

From the fear of being humiliated, Jesus deliver me:

Who would want to be humiliated? Naturally speaking, no one would. But even though there is a natural tendency to have an aversion to being humiliated, we should not fear having it happen to us when we look at humiliation in the light of grace.

If you experience humiliation, this can be a very painful experience. We should all reach out to those who experience humiliation with the utmost compassion, understanding and care. We must help them carry that burden. However, on the deepest spiritual level, experiencing something that is humiliating is actually an opportunity for you to grow in deep humility. Saint Faustina said in her *Diary*, "Oh my Jesus, nothing is better for the soul than humiliations" (*Diary* #593). This is a truth that is hard to understand and even harder to live, but it's true nonetheless. It's a painful truth that purifies one on the deepest level. How? By stripping away every attachment to that which our fallen human nature holds up as good.

A fine distinction here is necessary. It is not that humiliation is good in and of itself; rather, it is that this suffering and the affliction it causes disposes you either to grow deeper in holiness by seeking only the truth of God, or to grow colder in anger and resentment. When you choose holiness because of a humiliation, letting go of all earthly esteem, then you become purified and grow in a single attachment to God as the one and only source of dignity and value. This is good. However, it is a hard lesson to learn and to live.

If this is hard to comprehend, then spend time carefully and prayerfully reflecting upon the experience of interior fear in your own life and pray that the Lord gives you insight and understanding as to the importance of being free from it, especially the fear of suffering humiliation.

One way to do this is to think about the person who has no fear of being humiliated. This person is in no way under the power and control of the humiliating situation. A small child, for example, is not very capable of humiliation and experiences much freedom as a result. Striving for this form of childlike freedom is essential because its graces enable you to keep your eyes upon the Lord through all things and in all things. It may also be helpful to reflect upon the person who may react in a strong negative way the moment they are humiliated. Reflecting upon the contrast of these two people will help you also to see the freedom that one enjoys over the other. You should seek that freedom as a quality that brings many blessings into your life.

From the fear of being despised, suffering rebukes or being calumniated, ridiculed or wronged, Jesus deliver me:

As in the above reflection, being despised, rebuked, calumniated, ridiculed or wronged in and of themselves are not virtuous. In fact, these experiences are the direct result of someone's sin. No one has a right to treat you in these ways.

With that said, it's also important that you not fear if this happens to you. The virtue is found in the way you react to mistreatment. If someone has a grudge, a dislike or even a hatred for you, you must not allow that to affect you. If they publicly rebuke you or even speak false things about you, you must not allow this to affect you negatively or to steal away your peace of heart. The person who lacks a *deep* humility will allow the hatred of another to bother them. In fact, it takes an *exceptionally* humble soul to be able to receive the harsh treatment of another and to respond with charity and mercy for the person persecuting them. This is not easily accomplished. Therefore, *deep* and abiding humility is what is needed. It's not just a matter of being freed from pride; it's a matter of growing deeper and deeper in the beautiful and powerful virtue of humility so as to be freed from this very imposing and oppressive fear.

However, most people will not deal with the harshness, rebukes or calumny of another very well. This is very understandable given our human weakness. Therefore, we should be very careful not to rebuke someone for being upset or angry when they are mistreated. It's essential that we help others and strive ourselves to respond to all harshness with forgiveness and charity. And the first step in doing this is to overcome all fear of these forms of persecution.

Jesus Himself is the perfect witness to this humility as He faced Caiaphas the High Priest and all those who mocked Him and ridiculed Him. He never allowed their mockery and hatred to steal away His peace. He never allowed their falsehoods to dissuade Him from the path of virtue.

The countless Christian martyrs are also wonderful examples of this depth of humility and freedom. They often saw their persecutors as gifts from God sent to help them enter into their final purification before receiving their reward of Heaven. This level of humility is exceptionally admirable and requires that a person surrender to God on the deepest level.

From the fear of being forgotten, Jesus deliver me:

The person who is "forgotten" may struggle with the tendency to say, "Hey, what about me?" Again, this is understandable. However, feeling this way is not the ideal. The ideal is to become completely detached from this form of fear. It is true that God made us to both give and receive love. So receiving the love of another is a wonderful gift. However, when this love is lacking, and one is "forgotten," the humble person will turn to God as the sole source of comfort and joy.

Let's also be careful not to look at this only in a negative way, only pointing out that we should be free of the fear of being forgotten. It is also good to highlight the value of being remembered and loved by another and to reflect upon how the humble person will respond to this love.

When a person of humility encounters the authentic love and concern of another, when they are remembered, they will not receive the thoughtfulness of the other as if they *need* this love to be fulfilled. Rather, they will receive it as a *freely given gift* of love that turns their eyes toward the goodness of the other person. Their first joy will be to see that goodness and love which is offered to them in a selfless way and to rejoice in it. They will discover the pure love of God in such an act and this love will draw both the receiver and the giver of love much closer to the heart of our Lord. This giving and receiving draws both persons into the inner life of the Trinity and rewards them with an abundance of spiritual fruit. What a blessing this is to both.

Moreover, if that love is ever taken away, the person who is "forgotten" will continue to love because he/she will realize that, on the deepest level, they do not have a right to the love of another. We never have a <u>right</u> to another's love, not even God's love. Love, if it is pure and holy, is always a gift freely given and never deserved. Otherwise, it would not be the gift of love at all. This does not mean we will never be remembered by another and loved by them. On the contrary, by being free from the fear of being forgotten by another, we are only then properly disposed to receive their love if they choose to freely offer it.

From the fear of being suspected, Jesus deliver me:

This is a particularly difficult affliction to overcome. When we are wrongly suspected, or even rightly suspected, we tend to respond in a defensive way. We want to lash out and fight back. In fact, it can be very hard to believe that we should not defend ourselves in a forceful and continuous way.

Though legitimate self-defense may be proper and even a duty at times, the key here is to overcome the fear that often accompanies being suspected by another. If someone suspects you of some sin, the most humble response you can make is to listen, examine your conscience and respond with truth. If they are right, then you should change and rejoice in the fact that this person has helped you to identify some fault you need to work on. If, however, after an honest and sincere examination of your conscience you arrive at the conviction that they are wrong, then you should also rejoice in the fact that their false suspicion led you through this self-examination and enabled you to understand yourself and the particular situation with greater clarity. Your response will be the truth, presented with charity and detachment.

You must avoid being put off or disturbed by their suspicion. It matters not what someone thinks about you if what is thought is false. An error of judgment should have no effect on you whatsoever. However, as it is with so many of these humble qualities, this is easier to talk about than it is to live.

The humble person will receive the false suspicion of another peacefully, confident in who they are and with courage. Though this is difficult, they will ultimately discover that this false suspicion gives them an opportunity to detach from erroneous judgments and embrace, more completely, the truth. Freedom is discovered when a person lives more fully in the truth. It also enables them to move forward with confidence and peace of mind to face the many other challenges they will encounter in life. It builds character and, specifically, it builds a humble dependence upon God and His truth alone.

The Full Embrace of Selfless Desires

Overcoming *selfish desires* and *selfish fears* is not enough for the perfection of the virtue of humility. Freedom from these desires and fears is only the bottom line. The upper limit of humility is to grow in the opposite desires and convictions that instead will lead to complete selflessness, enabling you to turn your eyes to the good of others. Therefore, when you overcome selfishness, and grow holy desires in its place, these holy desires transform your character to the greatest degree. The perfection of love is ultimately obtained when all you *desire* is to love another. And, prior to that, the perfection of humility comes only when all that you *desire* is humility. Humility is no longer experienced as a struggle to overcome pride; rather, it eventually becomes a great joy and forms the basis of your deepest satisfaction.

Let's look at the qualities of the humble soul who has not only overcome pride but has also wholeheartedly embraced humility with every fiber of its being and with all its desire.

That others may be loved and esteemed more than I, Jesus grant me the grace to desire it:

Why is it healthy to have such a desire? Why would we want to desire that others be loved and esteemed more than us?

The reason has nothing to do with us not wanting to be loved ourselves. It has to do with the fact that the humble soul has so completely turned its eyes to the good of others that it longs for blessings to be bestowed upon others far more than it desires blessings for itself. This is a completely selfless desire and draws one into the perfection of humility. It may be true that when someone has reached this level of humility, others will love them and esteem them greatly. And that's good. It's good if people do love and esteem you on account of your holiness. The key is to not only be freed from the selfish *desire* for that love, but to also have the good of others as your singular focus. It must be your singular desire that countless blessings of love and esteem be bestowed upon others. This outward focus is quite transforming of your character.

It should also be noted that in this humble and selfless act, you will be consoled by the fact that God desires the same thing for you! He desires countless blessings to be bestowed upon you and He will not let you down. You do not have to waste your time and energy desiring this for yourself. God will take care of you when you achieve this level of humility.

In order to grow in this desire, examine your conscience and try to discover within yourself a desire for blessings to be bestowed upon others. Be practical and think about the people who are a central part of your life, including those who have hurt you. Let yourself be drawn into a desire for their good and allow yourself to desire this more than you desire it even for yourself. Do not hesitate to let your desires become ordered in this selfless way. In the end, this desire is far better for your own soul than if you spent all your time and energy trying to obtain blessings for yourself.

That, in the opinion of the world, others may increase and I may decrease, Jesus grant me the grace to desire it:

The first thing to note about this desire is that, in reality, the "opinion of the world" does not matter. It does not matter what the world thinks of you or what you think of others. Nevertheless, fostering a desire within your heart that others will increase and you decrease is good because it not only completely frees you from the desire for worldly esteem, it also helps you to have hope that the world will treat others with the love and respect they deserve. This is, therefore, a desire not only for blessings upon individuals, but it's also a desire that the world itself becomes a place of goodness and be filled with respect for the dignity of all people.

Again, you need not worry about what the world thinks of you. It matters not. However, just as in the above paragraphs about esteem and love, it often happens that when you have a hopeful desire that worldly respect for others will increase, the world will treat you with respect, also. However, this is not always the case and sometimes the world will hate you even more. Jesus even said this hatred would appear if we follow Him (see Matthew 10:22). However, as in all things, this matters not. The simple goal is to have hope that others will continually be respected and loved by all people and to desire this more than you desire it for yourself.

Saint John the Baptist is a good person to consider as a model for this holy desire. Remember that John had become quite popular and many wanted to make him king. However, once Jesus came to him to be baptized, John said of Jesus, "He must increase; I must decrease" (John 3:30). Earlier, John had said of Jesus, "I baptize with water; but there is one among you whom you do not recognize, the one who is coming after me, whose sandal strap I am not worthy to untie" (John 1:26-27). John desired that Jesus be known, loved and respected by all people. He desired this for Jesus more than he desired it for himself. Interestingly, John's humility actually fostered much admiration and love for him in the hearts of others.

That others may be chosen and I set aside, praised and I unnoticed, preferred to me in everything, Jesus grant me the grace to desire it:

These holy desires continue to reveal the importance of keeping our focus upon the good of others and not to spend time and energy on our own good. If we can actually desire that we be "set aside," and that others are "chosen" before us, or that they be "praised" and we "unnoticed," or that they be "preferred" to us in everything, we will be living in a radically selfless way.

It's true that these desires will be difficult to attain and you may even find yourself coming up with excuses as to why this is foolish thinking. You may find yourself thinking, "Why would I want to desire that I be set aside or go unnoticed?

This seems contrary to my own good. I want to be preferred to others!" But this is foolish thinking. Desiring that others be chosen before us, preferred to us, and praised more than us must be our goal. Living these desires makes us more human and enables us to become who God created us to be. At the heart of being human is the desire to give of ourselves completely, selflessly seeking the good of others in all things. This is love in its purest form. Moreover, in living this desire, we actually do more for ourselves than we could ever imagine.

That others may become holier than I, provided that I may become as holy as I should, Jesus grant me the grace to desire it:

This final humble desire has an important qualifier: "...provided that I may become as holy as I should." This is interesting because we "should" become perfect. Therefore, in reality, this is simply a way of saying, "Lord, help me to become perfect but make it my deepest desire that others also achieve this perfection." Of course, desiring this will actually make you exceptionally holy without you even realizing it or having to strive for that goal of holiness. But that's the key. Holiness is not about you gazing at yourself, admiring your own holiness. Holiness is about turning your complete attention to the good of others. In this act, if you can achieve it, you will become perfected without even realizing it or desiring it.

Living Humility

By way of summary, the humble soul first seeks to eradicate all selfishness from its own life. From there, it makes a conscious choice to put others first. However, this is not enough. True humility allows the choice to put others first to eventually take over every desire and passion of one's soul. It is ultimately in the transformation of one's desires that the true perfection of humility is obtained. This is only possible by a grace from God, purifying the soul in the deepest way.

3

The Virtue of Trust

Do you trust God? One of the most beautiful prayers you can pray comes from the Divine Mercy devotion: Jesus, I trust in You. So do you? And if you do, what effect does this have on your life? How do you trust? How deep is your trust? How did you arrive at the level of trust that you have? These are but a few essential questions that have to be addressed if you are to allow your embrace of the virtue of humility to lead you to the second most important virtue on the path to holiness: trust.

If you trust God in the deepest way, then you have faith in Him in an *active* way. Having an active faith in God means more than believing in Him. Surprisingly, even the demons believe in God (see James 2:19). An active faith means that you believe *and* fully surrender your life to Him. You entrust your whole being to God and to His providential care and guidance.

Moving From Humility to Trust

So how is trust in God experienced, practically speaking? Let's presume that you have chosen to embrace the virtue of humility. As a result, you have begun to shed the fear and anxiety that comes from worrying about what others think of you and you have come to see yourself as God sees you, taking your dignity and value in this truth alone. You have begun to be freed from the desire for superficial flattery and you have begun to fully desire the good of others, even more than your own good. You are becoming selfless in your thoughts, actions and even desires.

This is good and provides the basis for walking down the path to holiness. However, these humble dispositions are only the foundation for what is to come next on one's spiritual journey. Humility prepares you to make the radical choice to put your complete trust in God and God alone. As humility grows, so also trust in God must grow. So how do you take this additional step of putting all your trust in God? How does a humble soul, who has turned away from selfishness, now turn to God in an act of surrender?

Entrusting yourself to God first requires that you embrace the fundamental truth that *you can do nothing good without God.* Period. Understanding this fact is essential to the virtue of trust. God, and God alone, is the source of all goodness in life. Without Him, you are left to your sins and to a life of misery. It is sometimes hard to believe that you are powerless to do anything good without the grace of God. However, the truth is that no gift, talent or quality you have is sufficient to make it on your own and to produce good fruit in your life.

You are powerless by your own effort to walk down the path of holiness.

Do you believe this? Believing this truth requires the most basic form of faith: a passive faith. However, believing this truth is not enough. Faith must also be actively lived.

Let's begin by understanding these two levels of faith so that we can then learn how to obtain them both. Though this may seem more like a theological lesson than a practical one, understanding faith is essential to living it.

Active and Passive Faith

Faith can be described as both *passive* and *active*. First, a "passive faith" is sufficient to arrive at the *belief* that God is the one and only source of all goodness in your life. Having a passive faith means that you know and believe this fact and you do not doubt it. This is a good truth to discover and it is an essential first step toward greater trust. Sadly, it's a truth that many fail to comprehend. So begin with this step and ponder this truth in your own life.

Once you believe that God is the only source of all goodness in your life, you must then enter into an "active faith" in God. Having an "active" faith means that you allow your belief, present in your intellect, to move also into your will and ultimately your desires. In other words, you must allow what you have come to believe to change you. You must make a free choice to let God take over your life and produce good fruit in it.

The result of *believing* in God and *entrusting* yourself to Him is the glorious transformation of your soul. God enters into your soul more deeply and takes control, guiding you day after day in accord with His holy will. Living such a life of radical trust produces good fruit in your life and prepares you to both receive and distribute God's mercy.

A third point also needs to be made to understand how an act of trust transforms you. Believing and entrusting yourself to God is not something you can do on your own. God must be the one who takes control and transforms you. It is only by an action of God that you can actually trust Him. You must do your part, but God is the one who takes control of your life and enables you to be transformed into a soul that is guided by His grace.

To offer further clarification, let's look at an analogy. Say you have a seed in your hand. You know that this seed has potential to grow into a beautiful flower if planted and cared for. However, the seed cannot achieve its potential unless it is actually planted. Additionally, planting alone is not sufficient. It must also grow and bloom before it achieves its potential and beauty. You can plant the seed, nourish it and care for it, but you cannot make it grow. The growing is something that God does by His providence that He has instilled into the nature of the seed itself. So it is with faith. We must believe that God alone is the source of all goodness in our lives, but unless we actively surrender to Him, day after day, moment after moment, allowing Him to take control of our lives, then our faith is like a dead seed waiting to be planted. Total surrender is like placing the seed in the ground and allowing God to take over, bringing that seed of faith to fruition. If you do your part, God will do His and will bring His grace into full bloom in your life. Therefore, having the seed in your hand is analogous to believing in God, the planting and watering is analogous to entrusting yourself to God, but the growing and blooming is something that God alone can do. However, God is always faithful and will transform the "seed" if you do your part.

The Invitation to Total Surrender

Trust begins when God speaks to you, you discern His voice, and you begin to <u>respond</u>. Thus, God is the first one to act by offering you an invitation. Your response must be 100% a free choice you make. However, it must also be 100% a choice God makes by way of an invitation and grace. Trust cannot be arrived at without a perfectly cooperative effort between you and God.

For example, consider a person who encounters the hardship of a year of struggle after a serious car accident. During those long hospital stays, this person will be tempted with despair, anger, doubt and the like. However, at the same time, if he is open to the grace of God, he will hear a gentle invitation from God calling him to trust Him more deeply. It is in these moments that the person must make a choice. Will I entrust myself to the grace of God and accept His invitation? Will I respond to Him and answer the call He is putting on my heart? Or will I turn in on myself in self-pity and resentment? An active faith becomes a *response* to God in moments like this and transforms hardships into glorious blessings. Therefore, when you experience hardships in your life, open your ears to listen to the gentle voice of God, let Him speak to you, call you to surrender, and invite you to let your struggle be transformed by His grace. The fact that you make the choice to surrender to God in the midst of this trial adds much power and merit to your choice. In this situation, the interior anguish and suffering actually have the effect of elevating the choice to trust in God to profound heights. The suffering one faces is transformed into a grace. Therefore, it's important to understand that trials in life offer us incredible opportunities for holiness. When you make the choice to surrender more deeply to God because of some suffering you are enduring, there is great value in that choice because you are invited to radically overcome self-pity, selfishness and pain.

Reflect, also, upon the person whose life is going quite well. This person will also be invited by God, every day, to turn and surrender to Him more deeply. However, it's important to note that the gentle invitation from God, in these moments, will be far more subtle and will require an even greater attentiveness to His voice. Why? Because the only motivation for trust in God in these moments will be pure faith. The person whose life is going quite well will not be pressured by any outside influence to hear the invitation. Rather, that person will be invited to surrender simply for the sake of surrender. This invitation may even involve letting go of some of the "good things" that are encountered in life. However, letting go of these more superficial "good things" will be done to choose that which is even better: a life of more profound faith and charity. There is also great merit in this form of surrender to God. It is different than surrendering to God because of a trial experienced in life, but it brings much grace, nonetheless, particularly because the choice is made in great freedom without any immediate motivating factor other than love of God.

For example, imagine that you have a wonderful marriage and a beautiful family. Your job is producing a large income and you continue to advance in your career. You are living the "American dream" and all is well. However, deep down you realize that there is more to life than this form of success. You realize that God wants more for you and for your entire family. You begin to hear God's gentle voice calling you to a more radical life of surrender. As a result, you make the choice to respond and begin surrendering more deeply to the will of God simply out of love for God. You firmly resolve to give God everything and are ready and willing to let go of anything God may ask of you. This is a risky choice in a worldly sort of way. What may God ask of you?

The real question to ponder is not so much *what* God may ask of you; rather, the question is whether you are ready and willing to give *all* to God even before you know what He may ask of you. The key is trust. Do you trust God enough to let Him take the lead? And if, at first, His gentle invitation does not make sense, are you willing to embrace His will and say "Yes" every day? For the person who surrenders all, especially when life is good, the future will become even more blessed in a far better way than could ever be imagined. Perhaps not in a worldly way, but certainly in a far better way since it will produce the good fruit stemming from a life filled with an abundance of grace.

Let's look at an analogy. Say your daughter needs surgery and you buy her a gift and give it to her as a consolation. This occasion of her hospital stay offers you an opportunity to show your love by giving a gift. However, what if you decide to give a gift to your daughter for no specific reason other than to freely express your love on some other day of the year without any immediate motivating factor? Which act of gift-giving will most likely affect her more? And which act of gift-giving is a greater expression of love on your part? Both are good, and both occasions bring untold blessings in their own unique ways. However, the freely chosen and unexpected act of love has great value simply because there is no motivating factor other than love. So it is with surrender to God. When the only motivating factor for surrender and trust is love of God, this act is of great value.

The important point to take from this section is that no matter if your life is filled with suffering, is going quite well, or is somewhere in between, the potential for you to surrender more fully to God is great. No matter where you find yourself, there is great value in responding to the invitation from God to entrust your life to Him and to embrace His most holy will.

Discerning the Will of God

One important factor in trusting God is knowing His will. Unless you know what God is asking of you it is difficult to say "Yes" to His gentle invitation. But what is the will of God for you? How do you know what He wants of you? What are you to say "Yes" to in your life? These are important questions to answer if you are going to live an active life of faith and surrender.

Jesus says in Matthew's Gospel, "By their fruits you will know them" (Matthew 7:16a). So it is with the will of God in your personal life. A great way to discern the will of God is to look at the good fruit that comes forth when you embrace one decision or another. This is a very helpful principle of discernment to remember. What good fruit should we look for? St. Paul's Letter to the Galatians offers the following good fruits that come with the embrace of the will of God in your life: love, joy, peace, patience, kindness, generosity, faithfulness, gentleness, and self-control (see Galatians 5:22-23).

If you experience the above good fruit, you should use this as an indication that what you are doing is in accord with the will of God. If you do not see these good fruits in your life, or perceive other unholy effects resulting from choices you make, then you should proceed with caution and conclude that your actions are not in accord with the will of God.

But beware! Sometimes you can misconstrue good spiritual fruit with other forms of fleeting satisfaction. As an extreme example, some people may find revenge somewhat fulfilling.

They may take delight in this or that action that gets back at someone who has hurt them. They may even see it as a matter of God's justice, concluding in a self-righteous way that they are in the right and the vengeance is deserved. Though there may be some form of twisted delight and satisfaction that comes through something like revenge, once you come to know the authentic Fruits of the Spirit, you will not mistake them for false representations and distorted pleasures. St. Paul lists the following contrasting works as indications that we are not embracing the will of God: immorality, impurity, licentiousness, idolatry, sorcery, hatreds, rivalry, jealousy, outbursts of fury, acts of selfishness, dissensions, factions, occasions of envy, drinking bouts, orgies, and the like (see Galatians 5:19-21). If these are present in your life, then you can be certain that you are not making choices in union with the will of God.

Another important principle in discerning the will of God is to look again at the virtue of humility and to look at the way that humility affects your desires. Ideally, if your desires are imbued with humility, you should be able to quickly and easily follow the will of God simply by following your desires. However, your desires are only a good source of discernment of God's will when you are humble. When you are humble, meaning you are free from selfishness and fear and authentically desire the good of others, then you can more easily trust that whatever desire is in your heart is also in union with the will of God. On the contrary, when you still struggle with pride and selfishness, your desires are usually a poor guide.

Prayer as the Greatest Source of Discernment

The most important source of discernment and surrender comes from prayer. It is <u>impossible</u> to discern the will of God and to surrender to Him without an active life of daily prayer. An active life of prayer is not the same as saying prayers. Clearly it is good to say prayers, to intercede for your needs and those of others, to join in formal prayers, liturgical prayers and the like. However, having a "life of prayer" implies something much deeper.

A life of prayer means that you have formed a habit of communicating with God over time in such a way that it becomes ongoing, sustaining and foundational to every decision you make in life. It means that daily meditation, faithful surrender, a healthy moral life, and a basic embrace of holy living has so affected you that you are living an active and real relationship with our Triune God throughout the day, every day. A life of prayer means that you have come to know the voice of God and are familiar with His promptings. This cannot be learned overnight. It cannot come simply by asking God to speak. Rather, it is something that comes slowly, as a result of an ongoing relationship of love with God.

By analogy, consider two teenagers who "fall in love." At first, the teenagers may not be familiar with each other enough to understand the various moods, words or attitudes of the other. There may be constant struggles with clear communication, and emotions may cloud the relationship. Compare them to a couple who has been married for over 60 years and has lived a very loving marriage with strong communication. Often times, very little needs to be said for them to understand each other. In fact, in some ways, the spouses may know the other even better than they know themselves. This form of knowledge takes time, commitment and love. As the years go by, the relationship deepens and develops.

The same is true with God and discernment of His will. At first, a new Christian may not clearly understand what God says and why He says it. However, as the years go by and the person continues to pray deeply every day, this life of prayer, based in mutual love, will enable the soul to begin to understand God and His ways more easily. God, for His part, understands us perfectly already. However, we are the ones who need a life of prayer to understand God and His will more fully. Therefore, in a life of trusting surrender, there is no substitute for daily prayer with God, lived day after day, year after year, decade after decade.

Being Transformed Through Prayer

Your life of prayer provides the context by which you meet God and encounter His holy will more directly than in any other way. However, your life of prayer is not only for discerning the will of God. Prayer must also become the foundation for every choice and every action in life. Once God and His will are encountered in prayer, you must then allow the rest of your daily living to be transformed by these encounters. Prayer alone must become the source of all you choose in life because prayer will be your lifeline to the will of

God. Hearing Him speak, responding to His will, and allowing Him to transform your life will be the fruit of an authentic life of prayer. Prayer changes you, because in prayer, God takes over your life. This forms trust and surrender.

The problem that most people encounter is that they say a few prayers here and there. They go to church each Sunday. They try to live a morally upright life. But they fail to daily encounter the living God in prayer. Saying a few prayers here and there, going to Sunday Mass and living a morally upright life are great. However, they are not enough. Every person needs time alone, every day, to do nothing other than to pray. This is often a difficult habit to form. It's so very easy to allow the activities of the day to steal away the most important part of your day. It's easy to go through the day, week, month and even through life without actually connecting to God in a deep and all-consuming way. However, it must be done if you are to become holy.

By analogy, spouses who spend time every day in conversation, sharing, listening and understanding, slowly build the foundation for a mutually supportive relationship. This is especially true when what is shared is done so in a prayerful spirit. When the conversation is harsh, rude and critical, the marital union begins to weaken. However, when the daily conversations are ones filled with honesty, respect, charity, mercy and understanding, then their hearts grow closer. When a couple spends many years together, sharing this depth of conversation on a daily basis, the intimacy and love they share is powerful and sustaining. The same is true in our relationship with God. When we form a daily habit of communicating, listening and understanding the mind and heart of God, our bond with Him becomes sustaining and transforming to such a degree that our life of prayer becomes the foundation of our lives.

Embracing a life of prayer is not something that priests and religious alone are called to do. Everyone must pray and everyone must become familiar with the gentle and inviting voice of God echoing within the depths of their soul through prayer. This is not an option if you want to become holy. And if you understood the value of holiness, you would desire this form of daily prayer with all your might.

If your daily prayer life is not one through which you encounter the voice of God, then this is a good time to do something about that. Start by setting aside some time each day when you can be alone and have no other distractions. Even if you begin with only five minutes a day, this is good. Everyone can find five minutes a day for something as important as prayer.

Prayer is ultimately a conversation that must become ongoing. The time you give exclusively to prayer each day must permeate every other part of your day. It first requires a willingness on your part to be honest with God so that God can bring order to your life. He knows every detail of your life, but by bringing the details of your life to Him in prayer, you open your heart to know what He has to say about those details and you allow Him to enter in and take control of those details. This takes time and commitment. Therefore, the first step is to make the simple choice to begin communicating every day with Him. Let's look at one general approach you can take to begin a life of prayer.

When you begin your prayer, begin with that which occupies your mind the most that day. Perhaps there is a joy you are encountering, or something you are very anxious about, or both a joy and a burden. Whatever is on your mind, begin with that. From there, turn your heart to the Heart of God and simply place your burden and/or joy before Him. Do not seek an answer or demand any response, just give Him that which occupies your mind and heart.

Too often when we pray, we want immediate answers. We become impatient. However, God does not usually work this way. He often remains silent so that we will more deeply surrender everything over to Him. As you daily place yourself and your struggle or joy before Him, do not expect an immediate answer. Trust Him. Entrust yourself to Him and leave it at that. Be attentive and wait for God to speak a gentle invitation to surrender to Him. If God does speak, you are blessed. If you only hear silence, then know that this is what is best for you in that moment. Allow yourself to grow in patience and continue to place your life in His hands, waiting for His gentle promptings.

If you do this every day, you will come to realize that God does communicate back to you in ways that are beyond words. Your "answer" will come in a way that only God can speak. Most importantly, you will have begun to surrender yourself to God by daily placing before Him that which most affects you.

After spending some time quietly, placing your daily struggle and/or joy before God, there are many other forms of prayer that you can pray. Offering a rosary, praying a chaplet, meditating on a short passage in the Gospel, or praying other formal or traditional prayers are all very helpful. Come up with an effective routine. If you are not sure what is best for you, try various forms of prayers until you feel drawn to one of them. But remember, saying prayers is not the same as praying. When you say prayers or meditate on the Gospel, make sure that it is coming from your heart and is an authentic communication with God. You don't have to go through many prayers, you only need to pray. In fact, one prayer truly *prayed* is far better than many prayers only spoken.

Another important factor in prayer is silence. Don't be afraid of silence. If, for example, you are praying a prayer and something in that prayer strikes you, stop for a moment, savor it, ponder it, and listen to God in the silence. Listening to Him does not necessarily mean you are hearing an answer. Prayerful "listening" is simply a way of being attentive to God as He makes His presence known. Prayer is not thinking, it's being in the presence of God. Yes, we listen to God speak when He chooses to communicate some idea, but when God is silent, this means that He wants to communicate on a much deeper level. Words are not sufficient at times. In those moments, God simply wants you to be in His presence and know His love. So look for gentle invitations in your daily prayer time to stop and be silent in His presence. This form of prayer will do more for your relationship with God than you could ever know.

If you can build a daily habit of this form of prayer, spending even a short period every day with Him, you will begin to experience Him taking control of your life. You will begin to trust Him easily because He will be the one enabling you to do so. Your trust will happen as a result of being in His presence. By opening up your soul to Him and by communicating with Him on a deep level, you will find that you do trust Him and that through your moments of prayer you are surrendering to Him as He enables you to do so. This will especially happen in moments of silent prayer. The communication that He "speaks" to you will be one in which He enters into your mind and your will and then slowly takes possession of them. You will begin to believe more firmly and love Him more completely. This is trust. This is surrender.

Trust in the Scriptures

From here, let's turn to the Scriptures for some insight into trust. The following passages should be read slowly and meditatively. Return to them and let God speak to you through them.

> Blessed are those who trust in the Lord;
>   the Lord will be their trust.
> They are like a tree planted beside the waters
>   that stretches out its roots to the stream:
> It does not fear heat when it comes,
>   its leaves stay green;

In the year of drought it shows no distress,
>   but still produces fruit. Jeremiah 17:7-8

Trust in the LORD with all your heart,
>   on your own intelligence do not rely;
In all your ways be mindful of him,
>   and he will make straight your paths. Prov. 3:5-6

O Most High, when I am afraid,
>   in you I place my trust. Psalm 56:3b-4

In the morning let me hear of your mercy,
>   for in you I trust.
Show me the path I should walk,
>   for I entrust my life to you. Psalm 143:8

"Amen, I say to you, if you have faith the size of a mustard seed, you will say to this mountain, 'Move from here to there,' and it will move. Nothing will be impossible for you." Matthew 17:20b

"Do not let your hearts be troubled. You have faith in God; have faith also in me." John 14:1

"Therefore I tell you, do not worry about your life, what you will eat [or drink], or about your body, what you will wear. Is not life more than food and the body more than clothing? Look at the birds in the sky; they do not sow or reap, they gather nothing into barns, yet your heavenly Father feeds them. Are not you more important than they?" Matthew 6:25-26

But he should ask in faith, not doubting, for the one who doubts is like a wave of the sea that is driven and tossed about by the wind. James 1:6

And we have this confidence in him, that if we ask anything according to his will, he hears us. 1 John 5:14

These Scripture passages tell us many things about trust in God. First, persons who trust in God are truly wise. They are wise because they have discovered that God, and God alone, is the source of all goodness in life.

These passages also reveal that God has a perfect plan for your life and that He will never let you down. You should not be afraid of following Him, because the result of complete trust is far better than anything you could come up with on your own.

Lastly, these passages reveal that there is great freedom in trusting God. When God is in control of your life, the heavy burdens of anxiety and worry disappear. The humble and trusting soul is not tossed and turned by the turmoil of life. Rather, the humble trusting soul is always at peace no matter what comes its way in life.

4

The Virtue of Mercy

When a soul has fully embraced the virtue of humility and subsequently embraced a life of trusting abandonment to God, the floodgates of mercy are opened. This chapter will reflect upon this experience of mercy from four perspectives. First, the mercy of God that personally floods this humble and trusting soul occurs so as to free the soul from sin. Second, once freed from sin, the soul interiorly experiences an even more glorious grace of freedom and new life in God. Third, the infinite nature of mercy cannot be contained within this person's heart, so mercy begins to overflow from this person into the lives of others through acts of forgiveness and reconciliation. Fourth, once the humble, trusting and merciful soul offers the mercy of forgiveness and it is received by another, a spiritual bond of true friendship in Christ is formed. Sacrificial love then enlivens that bond, producing immeasurable good fruit.

Mercy is meant to be received from God and given to others in a limitless way. Our relationship with God and the reception of His mercy must become the foundation of our lives. As we grow in love of God, the holiness we experience will become the guiding source of how we relate to one another. Each person God puts into our lives will experience God's mercy through us in a way that God chooses. As we remain open to Him, He will use us to form holy bonds of love with all who are willing to receive that love.

Mercy for Sin – Forgiveness or Condemnation

It's easy to think that mercy and justice are opposed. But they are not. Justice is what results from one of two forms of mercy: either the *mercy of forgiveness* or the *mercy of condemnation*. The mercy given to a sinner is completely dependent upon the disposition of that sinner. Those who are sincerely sorry and repentant are offered forgiveness. Those who remain obstinate and refuse to acknowledge their sin receive condemnation. Both forgiveness and condemnation are acts of mercy on God's part. Condemnation fulfills God's justice by issuing forth the effects of sin to call the sinner to repentance. Forgiveness fulfills God's justice by accepting the sincere contrition of the sinner and removes the sin. Condemnation leaves a person bound and burdened by sin. Forgiveness leaves a person free from those chains.

The best way to understand these two forms of mercy is to look at God and His love for us as it is revealed in Scripture. Here are two Scripture passages worth spending time on to understand the mercy of God as it comes in the form of *forgiveness* or *condemnation*.

Forgiveness of the Adulterous Woman:

> Then the scribes and the Pharisees brought a woman who had been caught in adultery and made her stand in the middle. They said to him, "Teacher, this woman was caught in the very act of committing adultery. Now in the law, Moses commanded us to stone such women. So what do you say?" They said this to test him, so that they could have some charge to bring against him. Jesus bent down and began to write on the ground with his finger. But when they continued asking him, he straightened up and said to them, "Let the one among you who is without sin be the first to throw a stone at her." Again he bent down and wrote on the ground. And in response, they went away one by one, beginning with the elders. So he was left alone with the woman before him. Then Jesus straightened up and said to her, "Woman, where are they? Has no one condemned you?" She replied, "No one, sir." Then Jesus said, "Neither do I condemn you. Go, [and] from now on do not sin any more." John 8:3-11

The woman in this story needed forgiveness. She was caught in the very act of adultery and was guilty of grave sin. The legal penalty for her sin was death. But instead of issuing forth condemnation, Jesus chose forgiveness. And in that act of forgiveness, He perfectly fulfilled justice through this form of mercy.

In this story, Jesus did not excuse this woman's sin and treat her adultery as "no big deal." Rather, by saying to her,

"Neither do I condemn you" and "Go, and from now on do not sin any more," Jesus was acknowledging her sin and His right to condemn her. Therefore, true mercy requires that one's sins be honestly acknowledged and the consequences of those sins be clearly seen.

One aspect of this story, which is not explicitly mentioned, is that Jesus knew the heart of this woman. He knew that she knew her sin and He knew she was sorry for it. She had been humbled and she embraced this humility. It is this humble acknowledgment and realization of her sin that allowed Jesus to offer forgiveness rather than condemnation. She accepted that mercy in trust. If she had had a self-righteous attitude by which she refused to acknowledge her guilt, Jesus' mercy would have taken on the form of condemnation.

Condemnation of the Scribes and Pharisees:

> Whoever exalts himself will be humbled; but whoever humbles himself will be exalted.

> "Woe to you, scribes and Pharisees, you hypocrites. You lock the kingdom of heaven before human beings. You do not enter yourselves, nor do you allow entrance to those trying to enter.

> "Woe to you, scribes and Pharisees, you hypocrites. You traverse sea and land to make one convert, and when that happens you make him a child of Gehenna twice as much as yourselves.

"Woe to you, blind guides, who say, 'If one swears by the temple, it means nothing, but if one swears by the gold of the temple, one is obligated.' Blind fools, which is greater, the gold, or the temple that made the gold sacred? And you say, 'If one swears by the altar, it means nothing, but if one swears by the gift on the altar, one is obligated.' You blind ones, which is greater, the gift, or the altar that makes the gift sacred? One who swears by the altar swears by it and all that is upon it; one who swears by the temple swears by it and by him who dwells in it; one who swears by heaven swears by the throne of God and by him who is seated on it.

"Woe to you, scribes and Pharisees, you hypocrites. You pay tithes of mint and dill and cummin, and have neglected the weightier things of the law: judgment and mercy and fidelity. [But] these you should have done, without neglecting the others. Blind guides, who strain out the gnat and swallow the camel!

"Woe to you, scribes and Pharisees, you hypocrites. You cleanse the outside of cup and dish, but inside they are full of plunder and self-indulgence. Blind Pharisee, cleanse first the inside of the cup, so that the outside also may be clean.

"Woe to you, scribes and Pharisees, you hypocrites. You are like whitewashed tombs, which appear beautiful on the outside, but inside are full of dead men's bones and every kind of filth. Even so, on the outside you appear righteous, but inside you are filled with hypocrisy and evildoing.

"Woe to you, scribes and Pharisees, you hypocrites. You build the tombs of the prophets and adorn the memorials of the righteous, and you say, 'If we had lived in the days of our ancestors, we would not have joined them in shedding the prophets' blood.' Thus you bear witness against yourselves that you are the children of those who murdered the prophets; now fill up what your ancestors measured out! You serpents, you brood of vipers, how can you flee from the judgment of Gehenna? Therefore, behold, I send to you prophets and wise men and scribes; some of them you will kill and crucify, some of them you will scourge in your synagogues and pursue from town to town, so that there may come upon you all the righteous blood shed upon earth, from the righteous blood of Abel to the blood of Zechariah, the son of Barachiah, whom you murdered between the sanctuary and the altar. Amen, I say to you, all these things will come upon this generation." Matthew 23:12-36

This litany of condemnation is quoted in its entirety to present the clear, powerful and piercing condemnation uttered by Jesus toward the scribes and Pharisees. Jesus says, "Woe to you…" seven times in a row indicating that His rebuke was one of perfect condemnation. The question at hand is this: Was this a lack of mercy on the part of Jesus by which He chose justice over mercy?

As explained above, justice and mercy are not opposed. Both justice and mercy work hand in hand. The way that mercy is given and justice is fulfilled is dependent upon the heart of the receiver. In this passage, Jesus' justice was fulfilled through the perfection of *condemnation*. The definitiveness and severity with which Jesus spoke reveals that the hearts of the scribes and Pharisees were completely obstinate. They lacked humility and, therefore, could not turn to Jesus in trust. They were not even slightly open to seeing their sins and repenting of them. Therefore, it was exceptionally merciful on the part of Jesus to issue forth this powerful condemnation. It was merciful because His sevenfold condemnation had the goal of converting their hearts by revealing their sins to them. Jesus' hope would have been that, as they heard this condemnation, they would have listened, been humbled, repented and sought forgiveness. We can be certain that if any one of them repented after this rebuke, forgiveness would have been offered. If, however, they remained obstinate in their sins, then God's justice would have been fulfilled by the judgment they received from this perfect condemnation.

Of course, this book presumes that humility and trust in God are something you are already striving for and, therefore, you are not in need of such an act of condemnation by our Lord. Nonetheless, it is helpful to be reminded of this form of mercy given by God to the proud and obstinate of heart, to help you remember the ongoing need to seek humility and trust every day. Even the faithful Christian can fall into sin. When you sin, are you willing to repent and humble yourself before God? If not, you will experience the same condemnation Jesus issued forth to the scribes and Pharisees. The effect of this condemnation was one of extreme interior suffering in the form of bondage to sin and its effects. And that's a heavy burden to carry. Nonetheless, this condemnation is an act of mercy focused upon the conversion of the sinner.

A Mercy Beyond Forgiveness – Freedom and New Life in Christ

Even though mercy is first for the forgiveness of sins, it does not stop there. Once forgiveness is offered and received into your heart, God invites you to share in the freedom and glory of His abundant life. This second level of mercy is found in the story of the Prodigal Son.

The Prodigal Son:

Coming to his senses he thought, "How many of my father's hired workers have more than enough food to eat, but here am I, dying from hunger. I shall get up and go to my father and I shall say to him, 'Father, I have sinned against heaven and against you. I no longer deserve to be called your son; treat me as you would treat one of your hired workers.'" So he got up and went back to his father. While he was still a long way off, his father caught sight of him, and was filled with compassion. He ran to his son, embraced him and kissed him. His son said to him, "Father, I have sinned against heaven and against you; I no longer deserve to be called your son." But his father ordered his servants, "Quickly bring the finest robe and put it on him; put a ring on his finger and sandals on his feet. Take the fattened calf and slaughter it. Then let us celebrate with a feast, because this son of mine was dead, and has come to life again; he was lost, and has been found." Then the celebration began. Luke 15:18-24

This passage reveals the son coming to his senses after experiencing the effects of his disordered living and making the conscious choice to apologize to his father. He is partly motivated by his desperate state of life and lack of food. He is also motivated by a realization that he has sinned and that his father is merciful.

Though his sorrow and contrition may not be perfect, they are enough to receive the immediate gift of forgiveness from his father. However, this passage reveals much more than a simple act of forgiveness. The father not only forgives, he also invites his son to share in the abundance of his joy. He does so by clothing him in the finest robe, by putting a ring on his finger, by killing the fattened calf and by celebrating with a great feast. The son had come to the father hoping only for forgiveness and basic sustenance. The father, however, could not contain his joy at the son's return and lavished his mercy upon him.

The same is true for us as we experience the mercy of God. When we are sorry, even if our sorrow is not perfect, God forgives. He is quick to forgive in abundance, no matter what our sin. On our part, it can be hard to understand how easy it is for God to forgive. We often have very low expectations of His forgiveness and fail to realize that He wants to forgive far more than we want forgiveness. For that reason, it can also be hard to fathom that God wants to offer much more than forgiveness. He also wants to invite us into the celebration of His glorious feast. It's a feast through which we receive the infinite gifts of freedom, joy, peace, patience, strength and the like. God wants to bestow every good gift on us and He wants to bestow them in abundance. For our part, we only need to be ready and willing to accept all that He freely chooses to bestow.

One of the first experiences we will have once we are forgiven of our sin is freedom (liberty). We all have free will, even if we remain in our sin. But "freedom" (liberty) is so much more. Freedom is the interior experience of having our *attachment* to sin severed so that our hearts can then become attached to God and His holy will. This experience is like having a spiritual weight lifted from our souls.

By analogy, imagine that someone is in prison. One day, a judge shows mercy and grants a full pardon. There is joy in being pardoned but there is even greater joy in being set free from prison. Moreover, imagine that this same prisoner, upon being set free, is lavished with much wealth and has his former life restored tenfold. The new life that this former prisoner experiences goes beyond the pardon; it soon becomes a discovery and exercise of freedom as the new life that is given begins to be lived.

Therefore, the "feast of mercy" first involves complete freedom from sin, from guilt, from shame and from all the chains of sin. But from there, the abundance of joy that awaits is more than we can ever fathom. Too often we are tempted to hold on to our past sins, even when we are forgiven. Freedom means we come to realize and experience the fact that we are not the sum total of our past mistakes. We have a future. And that future is a glorious sharing in the new life God has planned for us. We are freed from the chains of sin and we are invited to live a new and glorious life in Christ.

As new life is experienced, we will begin to experience the Fruits of the Spirit. As mentioned in the previous chapter, these Fruits of the Spirit help us to discern the will of God. But they are not only guideposts to what we ought to do. They are much more. The Fruits of the Spirit are limitless and continue to increase in our lives as we enter more deeply into the mercy of God. They become the human experience of our new life in Christ. Traditionally, we speak of twelve Fruits of the Holy Spirit. These fruits are as follows:

> **Charity:** An ability to offer care and devotion in our thoughts and actions, with the same love God offers to everyone

> **Joy:** A spiritual experience which lifts us, strengthens us, and delights us

> **Peace:** A presence of great calm in good times and challenging ones

Patience: An ability to endure whatever may come, with peace and strength and without anger or frustration

Kindness: A quality of offering thoughtful and delightful words and actions

Goodness: A genuineness in virtue and character

Long-Suffering: A strength when life's crosses are heavy and enduring

Gentleness: An even-temperedness, tranquility, balance in spirit, unpretentiousness

Faithfulness: A steadfast and unwavering commitment to God and His Kingdom

Modesty: A quality of seeing oneself honestly and purely, being respectful and reverent with one's own body

Self-Control: A strength of overcoming one's passions and desires and of resisting temptations

Chastity: A deep respect for one's own sexuality as well as others'

Take time to prayerfully reflect upon these blessings from God. Understanding them is a way of understanding the experience of new life in Christ. Each one of these fruits offers a particular manifestation of this new life. God desires to bestow all of them on those who are humble and trusting and have received the complete forgiveness of their sins. As you reflected on these fruits in the last chapter as signs for discerning God's will, reflect upon them now as blessings bestowed upon you so as to become immersed in the superabundant life of God's mercy.

The Superabundance of Mercy – Mercy Overflowing into the Sins of Others

Mercy must overflow from your life into the lives of others. The overflowing of the mercy of God from your life into the lives of others will happen in the same way that you received mercy. First, you are called to offer mercy directed toward the sins of others. Let's begin once again by reflecting upon a Scripture passage to put things in perspective.

Parable of the Unforgiving Servant

Then Peter approaching asked him, "Lord, if my brother sins against me, how often must I forgive him? As many as seven times?" Jesus answered, "I say to you, not seven times but seventy-seven times. That is why the kingdom of heaven may be likened to a king who decided to settle accounts with his servants. When he began the accounting, a debtor was brought before him who owed him a huge amount. Since he had no way of paying it back, his master ordered him to be sold, along with his wife, his children, and all his property, in payment of the debt. At that, the servant fell down, did him homage, and said, 'Be patient with me, and I will pay you back in full.' Moved with compassion the master of that servant let him go and forgave him the loan. When that servant had left, he found one of his fellow servants who owed him a much smaller amount. He seized him and started to choke him, demanding, 'Pay back what you owe.' Falling to his knees, his fellow servant begged him, 'Be patient with me, and I will pay you back.' But he refused. Instead, he had him put in prison until he paid back the debt. Now when his fellow servants saw what had happened, they were deeply disturbed, and went to their master and reported the whole affair. His master summoned him and said to him, 'You wicked servant! I forgave you your entire debt because you begged me to. Should you not have had pity on your fellow servant, as I had pity on you?' Then in anger his master handed him over to the torturers until he should pay back the whole debt. So will my heavenly Father do to you, unless each of you forgives his brother from his heart." Matthew 18:21-35

This parable puts much into perspective. It not only reveals that God is ready and willing to forgive "a huge amount" of sin in your life, it also reveals that you must subsequently offer the same depth of forgiveness to others. And if you do not, you will lose the forgiveness you have received.

The very nature of mercy is such that, when you receive it from God, you must give it to others to the same degree. It's important to understand that this is essential to the very *nature* of mercy. It's as if you must see yourself as a funnel of mercy. God will not pour it into your life unless you are willing to open your heart to let it flow forth. Any attempt to hold on to mercy yourself, without giving it away, causes an immediate end to this infinite gift from God.

Additionally, it's important to understand that the more you open your heart to pour mercy out on others, the more God will pour mercy into your life. There is a direct correlation. Understanding this fact should inspire you with zeal to be merciful to the greatest degree.

The first step in offering mercy is directed toward the sins of another. In a sense, you are in a blessed position when someone sins against you. It's not that their sin is a blessing in any way. Rather, you are blessed in the sense that the sin another commits against you offers you an invitation to forgive. This reveals the power of God in that God is able to transform the sins another commits against you into an opportunity for your own holiness and their conversion. You become holy as you imitate and share in the forgiveness God shows you. Recall the Beatitude, "Blessed are the merciful, for they will be shown mercy" (Matthew 5: 7).

Recall, also, from the beginning of this chapter, that you are only able to receive the forgiveness of God when you are sorry for your sins. When you remain obstinate in your sins, God issues forth His condemnation to satisfy His justice and to convert your heart. This same principle applies to the way you offer mercy to others. Though you must always forgive, you will at times encounter those who remain obstinate in their sin toward you. When this happens, the forgiveness you offer them must also take on the form of a holy rebuke of love. Your rebuke cannot be a judgment of their hearts, since only God knows the heart. However, it must be a rebuke of the objectively sinful actions.

The greatest rebuke of love you can offer another is to forgive them. By forgiving, you are actually pointing to the sinful action. You are not excusing it, you are forgiving it. You are acknowledging that a particular action is objectively wrong when you say that you forgive it. Some will welcome this forgiveness and true reconciliation will take place. Others will not admit their wrongdoing and, thus, your act of forgiveness will become a source of God's condemnation. But this is mercy! It's not a judgment of one's heart, rather, it's a judgment of one's action. In fact, without making such a judgment, forgiveness cannot be offered.

Ideally, when someone sins against you they will ask for forgiveness. In that case, it's much easier to forgive and fully reconcile. However, when your forgiveness is not sought by another, and they remain obstinate in their wrongful actions, you must "condemn" them by your act of forgiveness. From there, God will take over and accomplish that which He wants to accomplish.

The *mercy of condemnation* you are called to offer others will take on various forms. For example, if you are a parent, you will often be called to correct your children out of love. You must judge their actions and be firm with them when their actions are contrary to the law of God. You must also correct your spouse, siblings, friends and others in the appropriate way and at the appropriate time. However, correction always begins with an act of interior forgiveness on your part and only addresses the objective action.

What if someone remains obstinate in their sin toward you? How do you react? The following Scriptures are good guides:

> "If your brother sins [against you], go and tell him his fault between you and him alone. If he listens to you, you have won over your brother. If he does not listen, take one or two others along with you, so that 'every fact may be established on the testimony of two or three witnesses.' If he refuses to listen to them, tell the church. If he refuses to listen even to the church, then treat him as you would a Gentile or a tax collector." Matthew 18:15-17

> "Whoever will not receive you or listen to your words—go outside that house or town and shake the dust from your feet." Matthew 10:14

When you go to someone to tell them their sin, you must be careful to understand Jesus' words correctly. The duty of "fraternal correction" is not an open door for you to judge the heart of another. Rather, it is essential that you look only at the objective actions of those you are called to correct, and not presume to know their intentions. There is a huge difference between these two approaches.

Judging actions simply means that you consider what you see, externally, and address it in love when the action appears to be contrary to the law of God and is causing some form of discord. For example, if someone speaks vulgar and critical words about another, you do not need to know their heart to know that those words are inappropriate. Thus, your fraternal correction will not be a judgment that this person is a sinner; rather, it will be that the words spoken are not consistent with the law of God. Though this may be a subtle distinction, it is essential to an honest correction of another.

More specifically, say a friend speaks many harsh and inappropriate words about a co-worker. How should you respond? You should take note of these harsh words and address them with your friend. You could ask them more about their frustration and try to understand them more clearly. As you do this, if your friend manifests more clearly that he or she is filled with anger and cannot forgive, then you have an open door to gently speak about the need to forgive. In this case, your friend has revealed his or her conscience in such a way that you can address what was said.

Or, say a spouse speaks a critical word in a fit of rage. Once the emotions calm down, it is essential that this outburst be brought to his or her attention. It's most appropriate, and most merciful, to tell your spouse that the words that were spoken were hurtful. Doing so is not a judgment of their heart; it's a judgment of the external actions. Furthermore, unless these actions are directly addressed and healed, it will be difficult to reconcile and enter more deeply into a relationship of love over the years.

Another important factor in making a decision to correct someone is the consideration of whether or not they are open to the correction. If, for example, emotions are still high and frustration is quite evident, it is more merciful to wait to address these actions later. Sadly, some relationships remain continually hostile and, therefore, it becomes very difficult to seek reconciliation through correction. However, there must always be hope that it will eventually happen.

If you judge that the time is not right to bring up the action that was hurtful or inappropriate, it is essential that you, nonetheless, offer the mercy of forgiveness in your heart. And when the hurt is severe, the forgiveness must be even greater, even if reconciliation is not possible. Note that "forgiveness" simply means that you make an interior act of mercy, forgiving them in your heart. "Reconciliation" means that the person who sinned is sorry, seeks your forgiveness, receives it from you and, thus, your relationship is restored and strengthened.

Praying for the Mercy to Forgive

One helpful way to offer interior forgiveness to someone who remains obstinate is to pray for that person. However, forgiveness of one who has hurt you can be very difficult. It is not something that you can simply accomplish overnight. It takes much grace and surrender to God. And it takes much prayer.

Jesus never asks us to do anything He is not willing to do. He forgave, from the Cross, those who had just treated Him so brutally. The chaplet below is designed to help those who struggle with forgiving another. Pray it daily if this is you, so that God can free you from this burden.

Chaplet for the Mercy to Forgive Another

The following chaplet (which is different from the <u>Chaplet of Divine Mercy</u>) is also prayed using a rosary. The prayers are taken from Scripture. The first prayer comes from St. Stephen, the first Christian martyr. He spoke it just before he died from stoning:

> "Lord, do not hold this sin against them." Acts 7:60

The second prayer is based upon the very words of Jesus as He hung dying on the Cross:

> "Father, forgive them, for they know not what they do." Luke 23:34

Start with one Our Father, one Hail Mary and the Apostles' Creed.

Then, on the large bead of each decade of the rosary, pray:

> **Lord, do not hold this sin against them, for You are full of mercy and compassion for all. Please give me the grace to forgive so as to imitate Your perfect love.**

Then, on the ten small beads of each decade of the rosary, pray:

> **Father, forgive them, for they know not what they do.**

Conclude all five decades by saying three times:

> **Lord, Jesus, Son of the Living God, have mercy on me a sinner. Amen.**

This is a powerful prayer based upon Holy Scripture. If you are finding it difficult to forgive someone who has hurt you and refuses to reconcile, then start praying this chaplet for that person every day. You will be amazed at how much it will help.

Ideally, when forgiveness is offered by you, the one who has sinned against you humbly accepts your forgiveness, and reconciliation takes place. However, too often it happens that the person you have forgiven will not acknowledge their action and is, therefore, not open to your act of forgiveness. As a result, reconciliation does not happen. Perhaps you have prayed for a person (such as a spouse or a child), forgiven them repeatedly in your heart, but they do not accept your forgiveness, holding on to their sin and a self-righteous attitude. Sadly, when this happens, all you can do is continue to forgive. If this is you, do not get discouraged. Discouragement is a direct attack on hope and once hope is lost, a forgiving heart turns cold and angry. Do not let that become you.

When someone in your life remains obstinate in their hurtful actions, all you can do is pray and wait for the moment when they are ready to reconcile. Recall the earlier passage of the Prodigal Son. In that story, the father was waiting and continually looking for his son's return. He saw his son from a distance and ran to him. So it must be with you. You must continually look into the "distance" searching for any indication that the person you need to reconcile with is ready. If you perceive any willingness, be attentive to it and be ready to show mercy and forgiveness.

However, in some cases there may come a time to "shake the dust from your feet" as the earlier quoted Scripture passage indicated. What does this mean? This is a holy sharing in the mercy of condemnation. When obstinacy is deep, and every attempt has been made to reconcile, there may come a time when the most merciful thing you can do to another is to "wipe the dust from your feet." This does not mean that you treat them in a rude, critical and sinful way. Rather, it means that you let them see the effects of their actions in your relationship. You allow their apparent obstinacy to manifest itself in a more visible way. But this is mercy.

This act of "shaking the dust from your feet" may happen in a variety of ways. For example, it may be the case that the only appropriate response you can give to someone is your sorrow. Not in a passive aggressive way, but in a merciful and sorrowful way ("Blessed are the sorrowful..." Matthew 5:4). When obstinacy is severe, a sorrowful silence may be quite charitable. This is a way of manifesting the effects of the disordered actions of the other. A sorrowful silence becomes a "loud" reflection of the effects of another's refusal to reconcile.

However, be careful, pray, forgive in your heart and allow God to guide you. Again, passive aggression can easily take on the mask of this form of mercy. However, passive aggression is just that: aggression. And aggression is not mercy. When you are called to a form of sorrowful silence toward another, there must always remain a strong hope that reconciliation will take place. And just as the father in the story of the Prodigal Son stood waiting and looking into the distance to reconcile with his son, so you must always be ready and willing to reconcile the moment the slightest opportunity presents itself.

Hopefully, this above experience will not be necessary in your closest relationships. Hopefully, hearts are continually open to reconciliation. When they are, the abundant Feast of Mercy is waiting to be experienced in every relationship. And that Feast of Mercy is made manifest through the gift of sacrificial love.

The Joy of Spiritual Friendship and Sacrificial Self-Giving

According to St. Thomas Aquinas, "There is nothing on this earth more to be prized than true friendship" (On Kingship To The King of Cyprus, book 1, chapter 11, paragraph 77). The bond of true friendship takes place when the mercy of God is given and received in a way that goes beyond mere forgiveness of sins. True friendship is the result of two people being individually united to Christ and, as a result, individually expresses the love of Christ to the other. This form of "friendship in Christ" is something that applies to every relationship of love you engage in. Of course, you cannot be "best" friends with everyone you meet nor can you be friends with everyone in the way that ordinary friendship is understood. Time and energy limits our ability to enter into close relationships with numerous people. But you can establish a "true bond of friendship" with everyone who is living a life in Christ, even if that friendship only consists of a brief conversation from time to time. In that case, it can still be the source of much joy since it will share in the outpouring of the mercy of God. A "true bond of friendship" can also be established between those who get to know each other on a much deeper level. Spouses, neighbors, "best" friends, siblings, etc., are relationships that ideally also share in the holy bond of friendship in Christ.

How is true friendship in Christ experienced? How is it lived? First, recall John's Gospel: "No one has greater love than this, to lay down one's life for one's friends" (John 15:13). It's important to note that Jesus calls us to lay down our lives for our "friends." This implies that the ultimate level of mercy can only be offered to those with whom we have been reconciled and share a common bond with in Christ. As already mentioned, when someone remains obstinate in his or her sin toward us, it is not possible to offer mercy on this next level. Their obstinacy keeps us at the level of forgiveness and they continue to experience the "condemnation" of our forgiveness until they repent and accept our forgiveness into their hearts.

Once you are truly reconciled with another and are thus friends in Christ, you are called to lavish the mercy of God upon them. This is ultimately done in the form of sacrificial love by which you put the other first and love them with your whole being. It's a giving of your very self. This depth of sacrificial love will be experienced differently for different people, but it will always be a sharing in the perfect sacrificial love of Christ as it was perfectly manifested upon the Cross.

Specifically, it will always be a total and freely given gift of yourself for the other.

The first thing we should note about sacrificial love is that it is "sacrificial." *Sacrificial* can easily be misinterpreted as something negative and undesirable. This is because, on a selfish level, it is undesirable. In our selfishness, we tend to take rather than to give. But mercy frees us from this form of selfishness and allows us to discover a much more glorious way of living. Recall the Scripture, "For whoever wishes to save his life will lose it, but whoever loses his life for my sake will find it" (Matthew 16:25). Losing your life for the sake of Christ and, thus, becoming an instrument of His mercy is what you were made for. Thus, in the act of giving yourself away, you discover yourself and become fully human in a perfected state of grace. Doing so is the way you become who you were made to be. You become more human by living the way you were intended to live, becoming more fully the person God created you to be.

This depth of love shared between spouses will take on the form of mutual support when each spouse is looking out for the good of the other. Children will always be cared for and certain needs will be met when parents offer this depth of unconditional love to them. Within the family, there is a special duty to give of yourself in a total way.

Mercy, however, is in infinite supply within the heart of Christ. Therefore, God will daily inspire you to offer your heart to others in various ways. Though this does not give another the right to demand of you more than God calls you to give, your acts of mercy to every person will still be lived in a total and unconditional way. Very often, God will also bless you with certain people with whom you share much of your heart and life. When these friendships mutually share in the mercy of God, the fruit of these bonds are sustaining, transforming, uplifting and holy. Even Jesus had people in His life with whom He shared a special bond of friendship, spending extra time and energy with them. Think of the Apostles, Mary, Martha and Lazarus. But Jesus' friendship also extended to all people, even to those with whom His interactions were limited to a brief moment of time. He continually gave of His heart, sacrificially, to those who were open to receive His love.

The key to sacrificial love is not so much about the *quantity* of time and energy you give to another; rather, it's about the *quality* of love that is shown. The quality of love given to a "friend" in Christ must always be of the highest level possible. Even if it only consists of a brief moment of time.

Sacrificial love will also "hurt" in a certain sense. It hurts in the sense that this level of love requires a constant choice to humbly put the other first. It requires a continuous death to oneself to be a constant instrument of the mercy of God as it was made manifest from the Cross. Love hurts. But it is a pain that is also sweet. Its sweetness is found in the good fruit that comes from giving your heart away to the greatest extent. And when this "sweetness" is experienced, the sacrificial aspect of love is not a burden at all.

Another experience we may have that "hurts" is that of spiritual dryness. On an interior level, many of the saints have experienced a form of interior dryness in their relationship with God. God feels absent from them even though He is intimately present. However, this experience of dryness is so that the saint begins to love God on a far deeper level: that of the will. Their sight of God becomes darkened, they do not sense His presence, but they choose to love Him anyway and choose to live out His will because of love, not because of what they feel.

We may also discover this experience of dryness in our love of others at times. Parents, for example, may not always experience an emotional delight in all that they do to love and care for their children. There will always be a sense of fulfillment that comes from their sacrificial love, but this love may not always be motivated by a good feeling. In fact, when that good feeling is taken away, their love may actually become more holy and beneficial for their children. This is because this form of love is more sacrificial and done purely out of mercy in imitation of the Cross of Christ. It becomes more selfless and more focused on the good of the other. Charitable self-giving may often feel good, but when it doesn't, we should not be surprised or discouraged. We must see those moments as opportunities to offer our hearts in a more total and selfless way.

When you daily give of yourself sacrificially, especially to those with whom you share a spiritual "friendship" in Christ, you will begin to find that your acts of mercy toward them are deeply life giving and sustaining. The distribution of mercy toward another person powerfully elevates you to a glorious life in Christ. By doing so and by allowing the mercy of God to flow through you, His mercy first flows into your own soul. Receiving and then being an instrument of mercy has the effect of filling us with much satisfaction in life. Make this your daily goal. Look for opportunities, with those with whom you are reconciled, to lay down your life without reserve. If you do, you will find that the mercy you receive from God and distribute to others will have no bounds. You will also find that living on this level of mercy is the quickest way to walk down the path to true holiness.

As mentioned at the beginning of this section, "There is nothing on this earth more to be prized than true friendship" (St. Thomas Aquinas). And when that friendship is plunged into God's mercy, the Fruits of the Spirit are experienced within it. The delight is great, and the strength that is mutually received from that friendship makes every sacrifice of love worth giving. Seek to make all your friendships glorious in this way, especially family relationships, and God will be very much alive in your life, coming to you and acting through you in the lives of those whom you love.

The Path to Holiness – A Summary of Our High Calling

This short book offers reflections on three virtues that are central to becoming holy. All three are necessary, in that one builds upon the other. But the ultimate result of living humility, trust and mercy is a life that is both deeply fulfilled on a personal level, and one that makes a tremendous difference in the lives of others.

When we live a life of holiness, ultimately giving of ourselves sacrificially, the result is a happiness that is beyond words, because in the pinnacle act of giving ourselves away out of mercy, we enter into a profound union with God.

5

A Living Sacrifice of Love

It's tempting to think that if you make the radical decision to become holy, your life will be much easier. In some ways that's true. However, holiness and suffering are not mutually exclusive. In other words, committing yourself to holiness does not mean that your life will be freed from suffering. But it does mean that your suffering will be transformed.

Think about the life of Jesus Himself. He was perfect. However, He also suffered to the greatest degree. Suffering is not a sign of God's disfavor; rather, it's a normal part of radical Christian living within a fallen world. Therefore, suffering even affected the Son of God to a profound degree.

One perspective we can take is to say that the "path" to holiness is made up of these three virtues but that "holiness" itself is fully arrived at only when those virtues are manifested within the daily sufferings you endure, embrace and unite to the transforming power of the Cross. The result of embracing these three virtues within the context of your daily crosses is what can be termed "sacrificial living" or "redemptive suffering." This chapter will look at the ways in which someone who is living humility, trust and mercy will approach suffering in such a way that their suffering becomes redemptive and imbued with sacred power. Though these are deep concepts, they are real and are essential to understand so as to live them as you encounter the normal sufferings of life.

Why Would a Loving God Allow Us to Suffer?

Let's begin with a very basic but important question: Why do we suffer? How could an all-loving and all-powerful God allow suffering in our lives? How could God allow the innocent to suffer? These are important questions because they present to us what initially appears to be a contradiction. The argument goes like this: If God is *all-powerful* then He can do anything. And if He is *all-loving*, then He would want only the best for us. Suffering is not a pleasant experience for us. Therefore, God should eliminate suffering from our lives because of His perfect <u>love</u> and <u>power</u>.

If this basic logic holds up, then we have a problem. We know that there <u>is</u> suffering in the world and that even the innocent suffer greatly at times. So what shall we conclude? Does this mean that God is not all-loving and/or not all-powerful? Certainly not! God's "answer" to suffering was not to eliminate it in a simplistic way; rather, He did something far greater. He transformed suffering and enabled it to become sacrificial, thus "eliminating" it by transforming it. Therefore, every form of suffering we endure now has the potential to become an instrument of grace. And this is glorious! Only God could do something so miraculous and unfathomable!

When God created us, He created us with free will. And with our free will we are capable of either choosing love or choosing sin. That is what free will is for. We can love or hate, become merciful or harsh, be virtuous or a sinner.

It's important to understand that if God were to eliminate suffering in a simplistic way, He would also have to eliminate our free will. Why? Because our free will is ultimately the source of suffering in this world when we choose to sin. However, it is also an instrument of much human fulfillment when we choose to love. So if God eliminated our free will, He would also eliminate our ability to love Him and others freely.

But let's ask this question in another way: Could God eliminate suffering *and* leave us with our free will? The one thing God cannot do is contradict Himself and violate His own laws. Though He can "violate" some non-moral laws He has created (such as when He performs a physical miracle by suspending the laws of nature), He normally does not do so simply because we want Him to. By analogy, it would be like saying that an all-powerful and all-loving God should not want you to be burned if you put your hand in fire. Therefore, you should be able to pray to God for protection and then put your hand in fire and God should protect you from pain. But that's foolishness! Though God could do such a thing, He does not do it simply because we pray for Him to do so. Putting your hand in fire has consequences and God will not change that. So it is with sin and the moral law. Sin has consequences and God will not change that. However, He does offer to transform the consequences! And this is what happens when suffering is transformed by our choice to turn it into a sacrifice of love.

Suffering Transformed by Sacrifice – Redemptive Suffering

> "I urge you therefore, brothers, by the mercies of God, to offer your bodies as a living sacrifice, holy and pleasing to God, your spiritual worship." Romans 12:1

How comfortable are you with the idea of *sacrifice*? For many, this word evokes both concern and admiration. When we see someone acting in a sacrificial way, going to great lengths to give of themselves for the good of others, we are easily inspired. However, when we are put into a position to act sacrificially toward another, especially when this involves some form of personal suffering, there is often hesitancy and uneasiness experienced in making the choice. Sacrifice is noble and easily understood to be of great value. However, it's much easier to admire sacrifice from a distance than it is to actually participate in the sacrifice itself. Too often, all we see is the suffering that is involved.

For example, let's say there is a hostage situation in which a group of terrorists are holding you and others for ransom or for some other purpose. As part of the "negotiation" with the authorities they decide to kill someone to illustrate how serious they are about their intent. They look at the group of you and ask if anyone wants to volunteer to be killed so as to keep the others from facing that fate. Would you step forward? Of course, from a distance, the one who does step forward would win the deep admiration of others as a martyr. But when you are faced with such a sacrifice, it's not as easy to make as it is to admire from a distance. Making the choice to sacrifice yourself out of love is no easy choice when it involves great suffering on your part.

So that brings up a related question: How comfortable are you with *suffering*? Most will immediately respond negatively to this question. Why would anyone want to suffer? Suffering and sacrifice are different from each other but are related. Suffering is of no value unless it becomes sacrificial. As an illustration, consider again the example just mentioned of a hostage situation and imagine that one of the terrorists is shot by the authorities. This inflicts much suffering upon him but that suffering is of no value, whereas the death of a martyr is of great value. Why? Because in the case of the terrorist getting shot, the suffering is experienced as a just consequence of his actions. However, in the case of the martyr, the suffering is experienced as a sacrifice. Therefore, only that suffering which is freely embraced as a sacrifice is transformed and has great value.

The sacrifices of martyrs as well as all sacrifices we make in our daily lives have value only because they are able to participate in the one and perfect Sacrifice of the Cross of Christ. His is the greatest sacrifice ever known in this world.

He was the Innocent Lamb who suffered willingly for sinners. He was the Martyr of all martyrs. He suffered greatly but did not hesitate in embracing His suffering in a sacrificial way. The effects of His freely embraced Sacrifice of Love was the salvation of the world. Thus, His Sacrifice bore the greatest amount of good fruit.

"Lackings" in the Sufferings of Christ

If we want to share in the glorious life of Christ, we must also allow our sufferings to share in His Sacrifice. In his letter to the Colossians, St. Paul wrote, "Now I rejoice in my sufferings for your sake, and in my flesh I am filling up what is lacking in the afflictions of Christ on behalf of his body, which is the church…" (Colossians 1:24). This is a deeply profound and mysterious statement. How can anything be lacking in the afflictions of Christ? However, it's important to note that St. Paul did not say that there was anything lacking in the "sacrifice" of Christ. Rather, what was lacking was only associated with Christ's "afflictions" (His sufferings). The "sufferings" of Christ are His sufferings. And although suffering itself has now been redeemed and imbued with the potential of the salvific power of the Cross, each one of us still must unite our suffering to that Sacrifice. What's "lacking" in the sufferings of Christ is the redemption and transformation of our sufferings in our present historical moment. We allow our sufferings to be transformed here and now by willingly uniting our sufferings with those of Christ's. We are invited to become members of Christ's body and in so doing we are invited to allow the sufferings we endure in life to become redemptive. "Redemptive suffering" is suffering transformed by the Sacrifice of Christ. It's our way of becoming a continual outpouring of the mercy of God by becoming a continual presence of the Sacrifice of Christ in our world.

Though the Sacrifice of the Cross is eternal, transcending all time and space, it becomes present here and now in our world when we allow His Sacrifice to manifest itself in our daily crosses. Thus, our daily choices to sacrificially embrace suffering and unite it to the Cross have the effect of perpetuating the Cross of Christ in time and space, making that one perfect Sacrifice present in every day and age and in the here and now. When the Cross of Christ transforms our daily sufferings, the "lacking" dissipates as His one Sacrifice is made manifest. Therefore, we can say that it is our high calling to daily "incarnate" the Sacrifice of Christ by embracing every suffering with humility, trust and mercy.

Sacrificial Living through Your Daily Sufferings

As true "sacrificial living" is embraced within the concrete experiences of your daily life, it must then be embraced day after day. Sacrificial living must become a habit by which you are neither scandalized by the crosses you encounter each day nor lose faith because of them. Sacrificial living in your daily life has the potential to ultimately transform the "burden" of the cross into the "sweetness" of God's merciful love, enabling you to remain humble, trusting and merciful in all things and at all times.

The Apostle Luke writes in his Gospel that Jesus said to all, "If anyone wishes to come after me, he must deny himself and take up his cross daily and follow me" (Luke 9:23). But do you know what your daily cross is? Do you understand why you suffer daily? Before you can properly offer it as a sacrifice, you may find it beneficial to consider the following three primary sources of suffering: 1) original sin; 2) personal sins committed against you; 3) personal sins you commit yourself. All suffering in life will fall into one of these three categories. By understanding the sufferings you will encounter from these three sources, you will more easily be able to unite those daily encounters to the Cross to experience the high calling of daily sacrificial living.

Suffering from the effects of original sin:

Is it natural for humans to sin, experience illness, fatigue, confusion, anger and eventually experience death? Most likely you would answer "Yes" to this seemingly depressing question. However, none of these are "natural" to humanity strictly speaking. But they are now part of our *fallen* human nature.

From the beginning, God created human nature in such a way that there was perfect order within us. Our minds were clear, our emotions were balanced, our passions were under control, and our bodies did not experience sickness or death. The rest of the natural world was the same way. Disease, disorder, and death were not present in the original paradise of the natural world created by God. However, once the freely chosen sin of disobedience took place by our first parents, the natural world and human nature itself suffered the effects of this original sin on account of the separation from God that was experienced by that sin.

It is important to understand this distinction between nature, as it was originally created by God, and *fallen* nature, as it is now experienced after sin. God created us and the world in perfection. But neither we, nor the world we live in, are in that original state of perfection any longer. The natural world is now filled with disorder (e.g., disease and death). We now suffer all the physical, psychological and emotional effects of a fallen world.

We also suffer all the spiritual effects of fallen human nature. The spiritual effects are what we call "concupiscence." Concupiscence is the unnatural draw we feel toward sin. We experience temptation and a tendency to act in a selfish way. Our first parents did not experience this tendency in the state of Original Innocence, which makes their original choice to sin (Original Sin) quite grave. They made a completely free choice to turn from God. As a result, all of creation fell into disarray. Regarding the spiritual effects of the fall, we, the descendants of Adam and Eve, now find it difficult not to sin. We experience much internal turmoil and confusion and, as a result, often sin ourselves.

Recall, again, the words of St. Paul quoted in Chapter Two, "So, then, I discover the principle that when I want to do right, evil is at hand. For I take delight in the law of God, in my inner self, but I see in my members another principle at war with the law of my mind, taking me captive to the law of sin that dwells in my members" (Romans 7:21-23). St. Paul speaks in this passage of his interior experience of concupiscence. This internal struggle within his fallen human nature is an affliction stemming from original sin. It is also an experience we all have on a daily basis.

Reflect, also, upon the very real struggle you have with disordered and confused thinking. Our minds are not able to make sense of life without grace. This mental struggle we all experience is also because of our fallen human nature and brings with it human suffering in the form of mental anguish, anxiety, emotional distress and the like.

Physical suffering is also a result of our fallen nature. Take, for example, the painful experience of a serious illness. In the state of Original Innocence, our first parents did not suffer any bodily disease and the suffering that results from it. Suffering and death were not the original intent of God in His design of humanity. We were originally created to live eternally.

The practical question is this: How do you embrace these forms of suffering that have resulted from fallen human nature and are clearly unavoidable so as to allow God to transform them? Though the answer is simple in its explanation, it is not easy to live until a strong habit of sacrificial living is formed. Therefore, the answer to this question is to return to the three virtues of humility, trust and mercy and seek to keep them alive in your life in the midst of anything you endure. These virtues will enable you to do more than eliminate these forms of sufferings from your life. They will enable you to "eliminate" these sufferings by healing and elevating the root cause. These virtues will clarify your thinking, strengthen your will and enable you to make the daily choice to embrace the effects of sin in a sacrificial way.

For example, let's say you encounter a serious illness which ultimately will result in death. The illness inflicts upon you several months of suffering. What are you to do? Some will become consumed in anger, self-pity and despair. Some will seek a quicker way out through euthanasia. Others, though, will embrace every suffering that this illness inflicts, humble themselves day after day, entrust themselves to God more fully than ever before, and turn their eyes to loved ones to comfort them and shed mercy upon them. Though despair, anger and self-pity are understandable to one degree or another, it must be understood that they are not the ideal to achieve. The ideal is to allow the suffering you endure to perfect the virtues of humility, trust and mercy in your life in such a way that your suffering is transformed and much grace flows from your life as a result.

The holy embrace of suffering and death, in this case, produces an abundance of good fruit in your life and in the lives of those who love you. The rejection of suffering, in this case, will result in more suffering. This is much easier to speak about than to live. However, if you seek to live humility, trust and mercy throughout your life, especially when you encounter a serious suffering in your life, it will be much easier to continue down the road of virtue and freedom. Those habits you have formed will elevate your new and intense suffering to the level of redemptive suffering as it becomes an act of sacrificial love. As a result, much grace will flow through you into the lives of those whom you encounter every day.

Suffering on account of the sins of another:

Suffering can also occur as a result of the sins of other people. Some sins can directly involve you with the purposeful intent of bringing suffering to your life, while other sins can indirectly involve you but still bring you suffering as an unintended consequence.

One example of the latter (suffering as an unintended consequence) could be the implementation of an unjust law. An unjust law originates in the mind and free will choice of a legislator and, thus, is ultimately the result of someone's personal sin (or perhaps the sin of several people). Over time, if that law causes you some undue injury, you are suffering because of the other's sin. Other examples of suffering indirectly caused by the sins of another are as follows: 1) A drunk driver causes an accident and does you harm; 2) A financial advisor is negligent in the care of a company's retirement plan and you lose much of your own savings; 3) Your spouse breaks the law and is sent to jail causing much hurt to your whole family. Of course, there are many other scenarios in which sins of others unintentionally cause others harm.

Sadly, sometimes the sins of others are purposefully directed toward you with the direct intent of doing you harm. For example, let's say you lose your job on account of the hatred of your boss. He is an unhappy man who dislikes you for no reason. As a result, he decides to inflict this suffering upon you by firing you and causing much hurt in your life and that of your family. By experiencing such an abuse, you have a choice to make. Either you will lash out in hatred and a desire for vengeance, or you will allow the suffering imposed upon you to "make up" what is "lacking" in the sufferings of Christ. It's important to note that your choice to unite this suffering to the Cross of Christ is not the same as saying the abuse is OK. On the contrary, by uniting it to the Cross you are acknowledging it as an unjust persecution. But when you choose to face this injustice with mercy and forgiveness and keep your eyes on the will of God, you rob the injustice done to you of its power. Furthermore, you allow this injustice, caused by the sin of your boss, to be changed. The evil is now a source of grace and mercy in our world on account of your choice to invite grace and mercy into that painful situation. By this act, you make present, in time and space, the sacrificial love of Christ Himself.

Some other obvious examples of direct sins against you would be: 1) Someone steals from you; 2) Someone verbally or physically harms you out of anger or malice; 3) Someone lies about you with the intent to do damage to your good name. In these cases, the pain inflicted will tempt most people to turn away from the virtues of humility, trust and mercy. The immediate reaction to these unjust injuries may be anger. And although anger is understandable, you need to be careful not to sulk in this injury or to turn to hatred or despair.

The person living humility, trust and mercy will more easily be able to respond to the sins of another with the Beatitudes:

> "Blessed are they who are persecuted for the sake of righteousness, for theirs is the kingdom of heaven. Blessed are you when they insult you and persecute you and utter every kind of evil against you [falsely] because of me. Rejoice and be glad, for your reward will be great in heaven. Thus they persecuted the prophets who were before you." Matthew 5:10-12

Refer back to Chapter Four in this book regarding the mercy you are called to offer others when they sin against you. The purpose of this chapter and this reflection is to help you reflect upon how sins committed against you can also become transformed into sacrificial love. It is not easy to refrain from anger in cases where the sins of others harm you, unless you have deeply formed the habits of humility, trust and mercy. But when these habits transform the unjust suffering you endure, that injury will be robbed of its power to weigh you down. This will be the case even if the person who sinned against you does not repent. Nonetheless, you will remain free to love and "rejoice" in life and stay on the path to holiness, regardless of anything you suffer unjustly. Thus, in this high calling of sacrificial love, the unjust suffering you endure actually produces more good fruit in the world than if you were never sinned against in the first place. This reveals that God's will is not ultimately robbed of it's power by the sins of others when His saints allow that sin to be transformed in their lives.

Suffering on account of your own sin:

The worst form of suffering you can endure in this life is the suffering you bring upon yourself because of the personal sins you commit. This suffering is always painful because sin has the direct effect of separating you from God, the source of all joy and fulfillment. When you fail to repent of your sin, your sin is of no value and continues to inflict upon you deep personal suffering. However, when you do repent, even the suffering that your sin inflicts upon you can be transformed into grace because of the mercy of God. However, the suffering that results from your personal sins cannot be transformed into sacrificial living until you repent of your sins and you are reconciled with God. If your sin is committed toward another, there must be repentance before the sin you committed can be transformed and elevated to the level of sacrificial living.

As an example, imagine that you struggle with anger and you allow that anger to fester and grow until it manifests itself in such a serious way that you do great damage to the ones you love. When the sin of anger is directed at your loved ones, especially when this happens in a habitual way, you do great damage to those relationships. Though your relationships will suffer because of your sin, the most serious harm you do is to yourself. That's not pointed out to lessen the concern about the harm you inflict upon others; rather, it's pointed out to make it clear that sin is irrational even from a selfish point of view because of the damage it does to your own soul.

The good news is that if you are able to sincerely repent, express that sorrow, and authentically change your life, God can do great things with the past hurt. It is even more glorious when your sorrow is expressed, is subsequently received and the anger is replaced by a new and habitual virtue of mercy toward those whom you have hurt. When this happens, God cannot only heal old wounds, He can even transform those wounds into new sources of love. This is especially due to the fact that the forgiveness of past wounds requires a tremendous amount of mercy on your part and on the part of the person you have hurt. However, if that mercy is mutually exchanged, the new depth of mercy shared, because of the past sins, is truly sacrificial and elevates the relationship to newfound levels of love.

This is not easy since sin requires great humility, trust and mercy to be transformed. But if it happens, the new level of sacrificial love that is shared will strengthen your relationship to the point that it becomes stronger than if mercy never had to be offered. As we say in the Easter Proclamation at Mass, "Oh happy fault, that won for us so great a redeemer!"

The same is true in your relationship with God. Though sin is never desirable, it's consoling to know that, when you fall, if you get back up, repent and truly change, you will be stronger and will love God with a new depth. Sin itself, and the suffering it inflicts, can and must be transformed.

When the sins you commit have long-term effects (for example, resulting in a prison sentence, a civil divorce, the permanent loss of a friendship, etc.), God invites you not to brew over that hurt, remaining in sorrow and shame. Instead,

He invites you to daily unite that ongoing suffering to Him and His Cross. In this case, the ongoing suffering has the effect of becoming an ongoing source of sacrifice and, therefore, an ongoing act of humility, trust and mercy in your life.

One Mysterious Source of Interior Suffering

It needs to be pointed out that there is also another form of interior suffering that sometimes affects those striving for holiness. This is the spiritual suffering of interior darkness. Recall Jesus' words on the Cross, "My God, my God, why have you forsaken me?" (Matthew 27:46b). While on the Cross, Jesus experienced a deep inner darkness and a human experience of separation from the Father. As a result, He cried out, praying Psalm 22. When you read that entire Psalm, it is clear that the conclusion to that prayer is one of faith in the midst of apparent abandonment from God. By embracing this human experience, which brought with it extreme interior suffering, Jesus perfected human nature in the area of faith, allowing us to know, with deep conviction, that God never abandons us.

At times, God will remain silent to certain people who seek Him. Of course, He is always there and would never leave them. Yet, He remains silent, inflicting a deep suffering on the individuals because of His perceived absence, to give them the opportunity to perfect their faith. In those moments, they are invited to remain humble, exchanging all their personal fears and selfish desires for what God knows is best for them. The goal is to deepen the personal trust in God in a way that could never happen if His consoling presence were continually "felt." It gives the opportunity to receive His mercy in the purest and fullest amount, and to unite human sufferings to the one Sacrifice of Christ.

This is a grace and, specifically, it's a grace that comes to certain individuals because of a spiritual affliction coming directly from God. God would not offer such an affliction to one who would not benefit from it. But if you remember that suffering is now redeemed and imbued with great spiritual power, then you will understand that God's choice, at times, to directly inflict a spiritual suffering upon these individuals is done only so as to make them an even greater instrument of His grace in the world. You should not be too concerned about this, however, since God knows what you need when you need it. And this form of suffering will only be offered when it is of direct benefit to the sanctification of your soul and the souls of others.

St. John of the Cross is the great spiritual master and Doctor of the Church who wrote on this spiritual experience most clearly. His books "Ascent to Mount Carmel," "Dark Night of the Soul," "The Spiritual Canticle" and "The Living Flame of Love" are the four spiritual classics in which he presents this profound mystery of God's purifying love. For example, in "The Living Flame of Love" he writes poetically:

> O living flame of love
> That tenderly wounds my soul
> In its deepest center! Since
> Now you are not oppressive,

Now consummate! if it be your will:
Tear through the veil of this sweet encounter!
O sweet cautery,
O delightful wound!
O gentle hand! O delicate touch
That tastes of eternal life
And pays every debt!
In killing you changed death to life.

This profound mystery of the spiritual life in which God purifies our souls by inflicting a spiritual wound of love is exactly that: a profound mystery. Nonetheless, it is helpful to at least understand that St. John of the Cross, St. Mother Teresa of Calcutta, as well as numerous other saints, have written on this experience in an exceptionally deep way.

The Unique Vocation to Sacrificial Living

In the *Diary of Divine Mercy*, written by Saint Faustina, Jesus revealed to her a unique vocation to suffering and the power contained in its free embrace. She was invited to become a "sacrifice of living love." Though this spiritual conference may be shocking at first, read it carefully and be open to the deep power of its message. The rest of this chapter will be spent reflecting upon this high calling of love in detail.

Conference on Sacrifice and Prayer

My daughter, I want to instruct you on how you are to rescue souls through sacrifice and prayer. You will save more souls through prayer and suffering than will a missionary through his teachings and sermons alone. I want to see you as a sacrifice of living love, which only then carries weight before Me. You must be annihilated, destroyed, living as if you were dead in the most secret depths of your being. You must be destroyed in that secret depth where the human eye has never penetrated; then will I find in you a pleasing sacrifice, a holocaust full of sweetness and fragrance. And great will be your power for whomever you intercede. Outwardly, your sacrifice must look like this: silent, hidden, permeated with love, imbued with prayer. I demand, My daughter, that your sacrifice be pure and full of humility, that I may find pleasure in it. I will not spare my grace, that you may be able to fulfill what I demand of you.

I will now instruct you on what your holocaust shall consist of, in everyday life, so as to preserve you from illusions. You shall accept all sufferings with love. Do not be afflicted if your heart often experiences repugnance and dislike for sacrifice. All its power rests in the will, and so these contrary feelings, far from lowering the value of the sacrifice in My eyes, will enhance it. Know that your body and soul will often be in the midst of fire. Although you will not feel My presence on some occasions, I will always be with you. Do not fear; My grace will be with you... (Diary #1767)

There are two primary lessons we need to take from this passage above. The first lesson is that God calls some people to a unique life of sacrifice and prayer. Saint Faustina, a cloistered nun, was one of those people. She was not given this vocation simply because she was a cloistered nun; rather, she was chosen by God for a unique life of suffering, sacrifice and prayer for reasons only known to God because of His mysterious yet perfect will.

Saint Faustina lived in a cloister, spent many years with serious illness, was ridiculed by many of her sisters, and from the perspective of the world was more of a burden to society than she was productive. From a worldly point of view, what good did she do in this life? How was it that living hidden away in a cloister benefitted anyone. And the fact that she was continually in ill health and was disliked by many sisters makes one wonder if she added more to the well-being of the cloister or to its demise.

However, if you read the words that Jesus spoke to her in this vision, and if you can take them on face value, believing all that they say, then the conclusions are profound. Read, again, the beginning of that spiritual conference:

> "You will save more souls through prayer and suffering than will a missionary through his teachings and sermons alone. I want to see you as a sacrifice of living love, which only then carries weight before Me. You must be annihilated, destroyed, living as if you were dead in the most secret depths of your being....then will I find in you a pleasing sacrifice, a holocaust full of sweetness and fragrance. And great will be your power for whomever you intercede.

If you can accept and believe these words from our Lord, then it must be believed that the effect Saint Faustina had on the lives of many was extraordinary. Even if we separate out the fact that her *Diary* is now published and many benefit from the spiritual lessons it contains, the message that Jesus speaks is that the power contained within her hidden, silent embrace of suffering saved countless souls without her even fully comprehending it. Saint Faustina became a "sacrifice of living love" and, as a result, God opened the floodgates of mercy, imbuing her prayers with great spiritual power for whomever she would intercede. Imagine her joy in Heaven as she comes face to face with the countless souls who were saved by the hidden sacrifice she lived.

This is a mysterious yet glorious vocation that has as its center the mission to suffer and to unite that suffering to the Cross of Christ. This is so that the "pleasing sacrifice" of the Son of God on the Cross is perpetuated in time and space and becomes a continuous source of grace in the life of the one given this vocation. Not many are given this mysterious vocation to suffering and sacrifice, but some are, and only in Heaven will we see the power of the hidden sacrifice that they make.

The second important lesson we should take from this passage of the *Diary* of Saint Faustina, is that all of us are called to live the unique vocation of Saint Faustina to one extent or another. Though some are uniquely called to embrace sacrificial love in a profound and sustained way, everyone is called to be a "living sacrifice of love" in accord with their own unique vocation. And what's most important to remember is that the spiritual power that flows from this free embrace is far greater than we will ever know in this world.

Practically speaking, your daily life offers countless opportunities to live out your unique vocation to sacrificial love. To discover what those opportunities are, begin by reflecting upon that which you complain about the most. What is it that bothers you the most, angers you, causes you anxiety or tempts you to despair? Whatever comes to mind is the first place to begin your unique vocation to sacrificial living. Allow the power of the Sacrifice of Christ's Cross to transform the "burdens" into funnels of grace and mercy for the world. Know that these perceived burdens are ultimately what will enable you, like Saint Faustina, to have great spiritual power of intercession for a world in need. Do not waste that power on self-pity, anger, pride or passing consolations.

The Sweetness of Sacrifice

If all of this talk about suffering and sacrifice has left you concerned, there is good news that will be quite consoling. Heaven awaits! In Heaven, there will be no more pain or suffering at all. In Heaven, all sacrifice in this life will be transformed into eternal blessings with which you will be rewarded. The rewards will be to eternally experience the fruit of your sacrifice and to rejoice in it to the greatest degree. In Heaven, you will never regret the choice you made to seek humility, to trust in God, to offer mercy and to live sacrificially. Every burden that you freely embrace here and now and unite to the Cross will be a beacon of light shining brightly from your soul in splendor and beauty forever. In Heaven, you will realize that every sacrifice was worth it and the gratitude you experience will be abundant.

But there is even more good news. When you embrace a life of sacrificial living here and now, and when you fully embrace every cross, God will often bestow upon you what we may call "the sweetness of sacrifice" here and now. Recall the earlier quoted poem of St. John of the Cross when he called God's purifying action "O sweet cautery, O delightful wound!" This "sweetness" and "delight" applies to all forms of suffering when it is transformed into a sacrifice of love. Yes, the suffering you feel may still hurt, the sorrow may still be deep, the sacrifice will still be required, but your full embrace of suffering will enable you to delight in the Cross of Christ as you are carrying that Cross. Jesus' yoke is never heavy and His burden is always light when we embrace His yoke and His burden in our lives with full knowledge and complete consent of our will. In this case, our desires, passions and feelings will eventually be transformed and we will find great consolation in the Cross of Christ. At first, those desires, feelings and passions will remain in confusion and in opposition to the will of God. But the more completely we understand and choose the Cross, the more that every part of our being will line up and experience the spiritual fruit of our sacrifice united to Christ's.

Look at it this way: What did Jesus experience on the Cross? Was it only pain and suffering? Or was there more?

Certainly, as He hung upon the Cross, His suffering was intense. But on account of His free embrace, His suffering also produced perfect strength within His soul and His suffering had the effect of manifesting the perfection of His human nature. Recall these words in the Letter to the Hebrews:

> Son though he was, he learned obedience from what he suffered; and when he was made perfect, he became the source of eternal salvation for all who obey him, declared by God high priest according to the order of Melchizedek. Hebrews 5:8-10

Jesus "learned obedience from what he suffered" only in the sense that His free embrace of suffering, in human form, perfected human nature and made it possible for us to do the same by becoming "the source of eternal salvation for all who obey him." We can be assured that as Jesus perfected human nature through His obedience to the will of the Father, as He freely embraced the suffering caused by the sins of the world, His human nature also rejoiced with an infinite amount of joy.

So it is with us. If we want to "eliminate" the sting of suffering in our lives, we must embrace it. And though, at times, God will still inflict upon us the spiritual suffering of interior darkness mentioned earlier, we will come to discover that this darkness is a blessing and is producing great things in our lives and in the world. We will also be assured that if we persevere in our prayer, as Psalm 22 leads us to pray, the result will be the greatest spiritual delight that will begin here and now and continue for eternity.

Imitating the Free and Joyful Embrace of the Cross

This book concludes with a reflection from the book, "40 Days at the Foot of the Cross: A Gaze of Love from the Heart of Our Blessed Mother" (visit www.mycatholic.life/books). In this passage, Mother Mary offers us the perfect example of joyful sacrificial living as she stood before the brutal crucifixion of her dear Son. Though her heart was filled with holy sorrow at the persecution of her Son, it was also filled with humility, trust and mercy. Ponder the reflection from Day Seven:

Day Seven – A Lowly Servant of the Lord

> "My soul proclaims the greatness of the Lord; my spirit rejoices in God my savior. For he has looked upon his handmaid's lowliness; behold, from now on will all ages call me blessed." Luke 1:46-48

As our Blessed Mother stood before the Cross of her Son, would "all ages" call that a "blessed" moment? Was she blessed, as she says in her song of praise, to behold the cruel and brutal death of her Son?

Though her experience at the foot of the Cross would have been one of exceptional pain, sorrow and sacrifice, it was also a moment of exceptional blessing. That moment, while she stood gazing with love at her crucified Son, was a moment of extraordinary grace. It was a moment through which the world was redeemed by suffering. And she chose to witness this perfect sacrifice of love with her own eyes and to ponder it with her own heart. She chose to rejoice in a God who could bring forth so much good from so much pain.

In our own lives, when we face struggles and suffering, we are easily tempted to turn in on ourselves in hurt and despair. We can easily lose sight of the blessings we have been given in life. The Father did not impose pain and suffering upon His Son and our Blessed Mother, but it was His will that they enter into this moment of great persecution. Jesus entered into this moment so as to transform it and redeem all suffering. Our Blessed Mother chose to enter into this moment so as to be the first and greatest witness to the love and power of God alive in her Son. The Father also daily invites each one of us to rejoice with our Blessed Mother as we are invited to stand and face the Cross.

Though the Scripture passage cited above recalls words our Blessed Mother spoke while she was pregnant with Jesus and went to meet Elizabeth, they are words that would have continually been on her lips. She would have proclaimed the greatness of the Lord, rejoiced in God her Savior and savored her numerous blessings in life over and over again. She would have done so in moments like the Visitation, and she would have done so in moments like the Crucifixion.

Reflect, today, upon the words and the heart of our Blessed Mother. Speak these words in your own prayer today. Say them within the context of whatever you are going through in life. Let them become a daily source of your faith and hope in God. Proclaim the greatness of the Lord, rejoice in God your Savior, and know that God's blessings are abundant every day no matter what you experience in life. When life is consoling, see the blessing in it. When life is painful, see the blessing in it. Allow the witness of the Mother of God to inspire you each and every day of your life.

Dearest Mother, your words spoken at the Visitation, proclaiming the greatness of God, are words pouring forth from the great joy of the Incarnation. This joy of yours extends far and wide and filled you with strength as you later stood watching your Child die a brutal death. The joy of your pregnancy touched you, once again, in this moment of deepest sorrow.

Dearest Mother, help me to imitate your song of praise in my own life. Help me to see God's blessings in every aspect of life. Draw me into your own gaze of love to see the glory of the sacrifice of your own beloved Son.

My precious Lord Jesus, You are the greatest blessing in this world. You are all blessings! Everything good comes from You. Help me to fix my eyes upon You each and every day and to be made fully aware of the power of Your Sacrifice of Love. May I rejoice in this gift and always proclaim Your greatness.

Mother Mary, pray for me. Jesus, I trust in You.

For more books from *My Catholic Life!* visit us at:

www.mycatholic.life

22069872R00080